The National Research Council Committee on Nutrition in Medical Education reports that six of the ten leading causes of death in the United States are linked to diet and that more people need to alter their diets to combat these diseases. Research suggests that the dietary fiber found in oat and wheat bran can help prevent and treat:

coronary heart disease • appendicitis
colon cancer • gallstones
breast cancer • varicose veins
ovarian cancer • high cholesterol
prostate cancer • hypoglycemia
diabetes • hiatal hernia
diverticulosis • weight problems
irritable bowel syndrome • constipation
depression and irritability

Research suggests that the longer we delay changing to a diet such as a high-fiber oat and wheat bran diet, the greater the chances that one or several health problems will occur. This is true for children as well as adults. *The Oat and Wheat Bran Health Plan* gives you all the facts, information, tips, guidance, and recipes you need to help improve your family's health now and into the future.

THE OAT AND WHEAT BRAN HEALTH PLAN

Dina R. Jewell
AND
C. Thomas Jewell, M.D.

BANTAM BOOKS

NEW YORK · TORONTO · LONDON · SYDNEY · AUCKLAND

This book is not intended as a substitute for medical advice of physicians. The reader should regularly consult a physician in matters relating to his or her health and particularly in respect of any symptoms which may require diagnosis or medical attention.

THE OAT AND WHEAT BRAN HEALTH PLAN
A Bantam Book / February 1989

All rights reserved.
Copyright © 1989 by Dina R. Jewell and C. Thomas Jewell, M.D.
Cover photo copyright © 1989 The Image Bank
Cover design copyright © 1989 One + One Studios.

ISBN 0-553-28212-3

Published simultaneously in the United States and Canada

Bantam Books are published by Bantam Books, a division of Bantam Doubleday Dell Publishing Group, Inc. Its trademark, consisting of the words "Bantam Books" and the portrayal of a rooster, is Registered in U.S. Patent and Trademark Office and in other countries. Marca Registrada. Bantam Books, 666 Fifth Avenue, New York, New York 10103.

PRINTED IN THE UNITED STATES OF AMERICA

O   0   9   8   7   6   5   4   3   2   1

This book is dedicated to Cal, Jefferson, and Tiffany. They tested, endured, criticized, and occasionally rejected the recipes as they were being developed. Hopefully, they will also benefit from the "bran in everything."

Contents

❦ 3 ❦

The Different Types of Bran Fiber

❦ 4 ❦

Why You Need Both Oat Bran and Wheat Bran in Your Diet

❦ 5 ❦

How Much Bran Fiber Do You Need?

❦ 6 ❦

The Oat and Wheat Bran Health Plan

❦ 7 ❦

The Oat and Wheat Bran
Health Plan Recipes

Foreword

Dr. Denis Burkitt came to speak to the medical staff while I was stationed at the naval hospital in San Diego, California, in 1978. If you have ever heard him speak, you will never forget his wry sense of humor and his colorful presentation of a very important topic: the importance of fiber in the diet. His message was unforgettable.

At the time, however, the importance of dietary fiber was only beginning to be appreciated by the medical profession and the lay population. After I heard Dr. Burkitt speak, I went home to discuss the topic, about which I had only then become enthusiastic, with my wife, Dina. She reminded me that she had been telling me for years about the need for fiber in the diet, and in fact had been adding wheat bran to our food regularly for quite a while. She also showed me a collection of newspaper clippings she had been accumulating. She had known of Dr. Burkitt's work for some time, and announced that someday she was going to write a cookbook using fiber in everyday recipes. She thought everyone should be as enthusiastic about fiber as Dr. Burkitt.

Subsequently, it became clear to me that what Dr. Burkitt had said correlated well with what I had noted in my practice and in my own life. The prevalence of the diseases that he attributed to lack of fiber was overwhelming. These diseases make necessary the large hospitals we have in our communities, and occupy the practice of the general surgeon. Coronary artery disease, gallstones, hemorrhoids, colonic diseases (colon cancer, diverticulitis, and constipation), and obesity constitute a major portion of the diseases that keep a surgeon busy. If one adds breast pain, breast cancer, varicose veins, hiatus hernia, and appendicitis to the list, the time of the general surgeon is pretty well taken up. Hypercholesterolemia and its implications for the medical profession—hypertension, diabetes, depression and irritability, varicose veins, and irritable-bowel syndrome—must collectively account for a lion's share of the medical-care dollars we spend in this country every year. Increasing evidence suggests that these diseases can be treated or prevented by the addition of fiber to the diet.

Over the years in my practice I have seen many patients who suffered from hemorrhoids and diverticular disease of the colon who were "ready to have an operation" to rid themselves of their symptoms. The vast majority of these were pleased to be told (and subsequently find out for themselves) that a gradual increase in their dietary fiber would reduce the severity of their symptoms to the point that surgery would probably not be necessary.

The unfortunate part of the story, however, is that these patients and many others would have been much better off if the fiber had been introduced into their diets much earlier. As we get older and our systems begin to slow down (and we become much more aware of our own mortality), we begin to look for ways to improve our health and longevity. The symptoms will often respond to increased fiber, but the development of the diseases themselves would certainly have been retarded if we had begun the high-fiber, low-fat diet years sooner. Although it is never too late to start eating right, the real secret is to begin as early as possible—in childhood if possible.

The beauty of this book and the underlying health plan is its simplicity. So often one hears of a "health plan" that promises miraculous results but requires the patient to change his or her eating habits totally. Or the plan requires one to eat things that don't taste good. This is not realistic. Patient noncompliance is always a major factor in the failure of any treatment plan, and the availability of an easy-to-follow, realistic, inexpensive health plan that does not require a radical change in cooking and eating habits should go a long way to improve the health of the participants because compliance is easy.

Dina's recipes can have a major impact on your health, and I am happy that they are now available for all families as they have been for my family.

—C. THOMAS JEWELL, M.D.

Introduction

The Oat and Wheat Bran Health Plan is the product of many years of using bran fiber in cooking for my family. During this time I became aware of the fact that there was a lack of information on how to use bran fiber in the recipes that have come to be family favorites. It has been over fifteen years of trial and error plus much success with adding bran fiber to our family meals that has led to the development of these recipes and health plan.

I first became interested in the work of Dr. Denis Burkitt after reading several of his articles concerning bran. It was Dr. Burkitt's theory that many diseases and medical problems in the western world were directly related to a lack of fiber in the diet. In Africa, by comparison, where these common serious medical problems are rare, the people ingest a large amount of dietary fiber. Dr. Burkitt's basic premise was that our everyday diet is killing us.

On the basis of this medical information I bought some bran—which was not easy to find, since it was not as popular an item in the 1970s as it is now—at a health food store that catered to the few remaining flower children. I first tried cornmeal fiber because finding a recipe for corn bread is easy in the South, where we were living at the time. My family enjoyed the corn bread so much, I wondered how to put more fiber into other foods, because one can bake only so much corn bread. So I began to use wheat bran in my regular family recipes.

The first successes that I had were with my Aunt Honey's banana bread recipe and a chocolate cake recipe. I was surprised at how moist the bread and cake always turned out, and at how much more substance there seemed to be in the food. My family began to prefer my banana bread and chocolate cake to bought or packaged ones. We found that everyone had more energy, were hungry less often, and had active and easy bowel functions, all of which are important to children since constipation and stomachache can be painful health problems. I found that in teaching my aerobic classes, I had high energy longer when I ate my own foods containing bran than when I ate anything else. I remember that I often told people about the worth of bran in food, but just as very few people were listening to Dr. Burkitt, no one was listening to me.

I started cooking regularly with bran, and began to compile a list of bran-inclusive recipes. Spaghetti with bran was one of my most often used dishes, as were meat loaf and other ground-meat meals. As a family we always commented on how much better we all felt after eating bran in our food. As a matter of fact, when we would travel and not eat bran every day as we did at home, the first thing that everyone would want when we got home was some food with bran in it, or, as my group began to call it, "some real food!"

I began to use bran in "everything I could get away with," as the children put it, and found that I was always grateful for the fact that even the piece of chocolate cake that the children were eating as they raced around was good for them and their digestive tract.

It was about this time that my husband, Tom, told me how impressed he was with Dr. Burkitt's theories. I showed him the information on Dr. Burkitt that I had been collecting and told him that that's what we'd been doing at home all along. His reaction was "Was that what we've been doing?" I guess you have to be married to a doctor to understand how often his mind is not at home even if his person is; anyway, I had by that time accumulated many bran recipes.

It was not until we were living in Boise, Idaho, that I became aware that there was no cookbook or other instructional material available that dealt with how to use bran fiber in everyday family food. Many cookbooks had some recipes on ways to include more "fiber" in the diet but not necessarily bran; or there were cookbooks on how to change everything that you are doing at the present and start again with different food products in order to put fiber into your life; once again, not necessarily bran. But I could find no cookbook using a method for including bran in food that was as simple and as reliable as the one that I was using.

Tom began to use bran as a treatment with his patients, especially the many with intestinal and colonic diseases. He asked me to suggest some recipes in which bran fiber could be used with absolute success so that he could recommend them to his patients as he told of the need for more fiber in their diet. I supplied him with some recipe information, and soon his patients were asking for more bran recipes. I could see that what for me was a simple method of adding bran to everyday food was not so easy a process to many. So I began to write down my recipes.

At the same time I was in the process of completing my master's degree and felt that this information on adding bran to ordinary recipes would constitute instructional material. My adviser, Dr. John Jensen of the Education Department at Boise State University, agreed and sent me to the Health Science Department to begin my research. The Health Science Department felt that this information on how to put bran into the diet could be useful to their home services for the elderly program. During my research into the medical indications for bran in the diet I was amazed at the variety of serious diseases that were related to the ingestion of inadequate amounts of fiber. As my awareness grew through my research, so did the project which, coupled with my ten to fifteen years of accumulated workable bran recipes, qualified for my master's degree thesis with the Education Department. The medical information that I had accumulated on the number of medical indications for the need of bran in the diet was surprising even to my husband, who thought he already was aware of most of the indications for fiber.

When required to compile a complete recipe collection, I had to expand my easy-application method of bran to all areas of daily meal planning. This directed me to discover how bran can be incorporated in almost every area of cooking and led me to develop some of the best recipes in the book. It also led me to add bran to brownies, pumpkin pie, and even Rice Krispies squares, much to the delight of my young daughter, who, when she wanted to make some Rice Krispies squares, said, "I'll even put bran in them." She was surprised that it worked so well.

What surprised me the most in my research on bran was that children need bran in their everyday diets as much as adults and even senior citizens. I had thought initially that the projection for this book on bran fiber recipes would be toward people forty-five years or older, but I quickly came to realize that children need bran as much as, if not more than, older adults. Most of all, children need adequate bran during childhood in order to avoid the irreversible damage that can be done by a low-fiber diet, which will result in major health problems such as appendicitis, diverticulosis, irritable-bowel syndrome, constipation, colon cancer, and high cholesterol as well as diabetes, hypoglycemia, and other "adult" diseases.

My research also led me to see that wheat bran is equally as important to the full health diet as is oat bran. Much has been said lately about the worth of oat bran because of its ability to lower cholesterol; however, wheat bran is equally if not more important to the body, since it is the increased transit speed through the intestinal tract that wheat bran provides that is so vital to intestinal health. As you will discover as you read the following chapters, both oat and wheat brans are necessary for good health.

I want to point out here that I am not a professional cook. I cook for myself and my family out of necessity, not as an art form. I cook because we have to eat; therefore, I want the food that I spend time on to be able to go the distance and do the most for my family and myself. We all are busy; our three children (one each in college, high school, and grade school) are constantly running to their various lessons and activities; Tom is a surgeon and has a great many meetings to attend in addition to his own practice. I have been a fitness instructor for ten years in both California and Idaho. I currently teach aerobics classes at the YWCA, have a daily fitness show on United Cable TV, and do commercial work. Daily we all rely on the energy that we get from *The Oat and Wheat Bran Health Plan* recipes. I often recommend my bran recipes to my students. My husband can stir up two to three tablespoons of bran fiber in a glass of water and drink it down every morning. I cannot. I have to have something more palatable than that to start my day. So the children and I rely on the Breakfast Cookies and muffins to provide the energy to get us going quickly in the morning and fill in the cracks of needed energy during the day. I am convinced that bran, along with being a protector against many major health problems, is a high-energy provider. My whole family finds that bran in food provides more energy longer than any other source of nutrition.

The unique point about this health plan book is that the method of using bran fiber in the everyday diet is simple. The recipes are easy to follow and practical to use because they are recipes that you will recognize and already enjoy. Furthermore, the method of application can be easily applied to other favorite recipes of your own. I have found it helpful to keep bran in a glass container on the cupboard top. This way, the bran stays in your view and within your reach all the time. I urge you to do the same.

It is my hope that you will find *The Oat and Wheat Bran Health Plan* as useful in your life as my family and I have. As you take advantage of this easy-application approach to a full-fiber diet, keep in mind that as easy as it is, it still is a necessity to good health.

—DINA R. JEWELL

THE
OAT AND
WHEAT
BRAN
HEALTH PLAN

🙚 1 🙘

The Real Story of
Bran Fiber

BRAN FIBER IS A HEALTH BOOSTER

Suppose there were a food that could satisfy your appetite, has almost no calories, can lower cholesterol and blood sugar, and could reduce your risk of heart attack, high blood pressure, intestinal disease, and diabetes? This same food could help you lose weight, and could even play an important protective role against cancer. Wouldn't you say "I need that in my life!"

Fiber, a long-neglected food, has become a significant medical discovery and a valuable necessity in the everyday diet. International medical research has determined that bran is good for you; it is especially good for lowering cholesterol, for maintaining a healthy digestive tract, and it plays an important role in both the prevention and treatment of several major health problems.

1

Only in relatively recent years has the role of dietary fiber, once thought to be an unnecessary and even undesirable food by-product, begun to be appreciated in the maintenance and promotion of good health. Medical research now indicates that a deficiency of fiber in the modern western diet may contribute to a host of diseases that plague both the old and the young. In short, it has been determined that lack of dietary fiber produces low fecal bulk, which in turn has been found to cause or contribute to coronary artery disease, colon cancer, diverticular disease, appendicitis, constipation, hiatal hernia, diabetes, high cholesterol, other intestinal disorders, weight problems, certain other cancers, high blood pressure, and, possibly, depression and irritability.

WHAT'S CONTRIBUTING TO THE RISE OF THESE DISEASES?

There is a simple but very disturbing answer to this question. Technological advances have reduced and refined our plant food intake. Consequently, the refined food products that we all eat have brought about an unprecedented decline in the consumption of dietary fiber. The emergence of certain diseases selectively in regions which have been most affected by this dietary change has led to an enhanced awareness of the functions of dietary fiber.

The National Research Council Committee on Nutrition in Medical Education reports that six of the ten leading causes of death in the United States are linked to diet and that more people need to alter their diets to combat these diseases.

WHAT THE RESEARCH HAS DETERMINED

The lack of adequate fiber in the diet has been pointed to as the element that is responsible for a variety of health problems. Medical evidence supports the fact that fiber is a protector of the digestive tract and can help guard against a variety of serious diseases.

Research suggests that dietary fiber can help prevent and treat:

Coronary artery disease	High cholesterol
Hypertension (high blood pressure)	Appendicitis
	Irritable-bowel syndrome
Colon cancer	Gallstones
Breast cancer	Constipation
Prostate cancer	Hiatal hernia
Ovarian cancer	Varicose veins
Diverticulosis	Depression and irritability
Diabetes	
Hypoglycemia (low blood sugar)	Hemorrhoids
Obesity	Adverse effects of food additives

Dietary fiber, a plant-derived material part of which is resistant to digestion, has been recognized as having certain established homeostatic and medically therapeutic functions in human nutrition. The benefits of using dietary fiber in the treatment of constipation, uncomplicated diverticular disease, and various intestinal diseases as well as in the treatment of diabetes and high cholesterol levels are becoming well-established. Since 1970 the information about dietary fiber has grown and become scientifically and clinically accepted. Even though more needs to be known about some of the more complex effects of fiber, the medical community now recognizes that dietary fiber is an important element in nutrition.

THE DIETARY BASIS FOR BRAN FIBER

The hypothesis that dietary fiber may be a protective factor in human disease was first proposed by Dr. Denis Burkitt, a member of Britain's Medical Research Council, in 1971, after many years of observation of dietary fiber in Africa. This hypothesis was subsequently supported by Dr. Burkitt with data on the distribution of fiber consumption in different populations. Dr. Burkitt's research concluded that dietary fiber is essential for good health.

Dr. Burkitt, who spent twenty years as a surgeon in Uganda, suggested that fiber was a protector of the digestive tract and that lack of fiber in the diet can lead to the development of a variety of serious diseases. Most important, he also argued that each of these diseases is in fact a result of consuming fiber-depleted diets. Dr. Burkitt as well as others began to discern the possible significance of fiber by realizing that many of the diseases that were becoming increasingly common in Britain, the United States, and much of the western world were rarely found in Africa.

Appendicitis, for example, is a fairly common abdominal surgical emergency that necessitates the removal of 300,000 appendixes in the United States each year. Yet Dr. Burkitt found that appendicitis was almost nonexistent among the African villagers that he had been studying. Likewise, in the west, after age forty, one-half of all Americans develop diverticular disease. But in twenty years in Africa Dr. Burkitt did not see a single case of diverticular disease, as he reported in *Gastroenterology* in 1977. Furthermore, coronary artery disease, the heart-attack promoter that is responsible for one third of all deaths in the United States, is rarely seen in most of Africa; and colon cancer, while striking more than 100,000 victims a year in the United States alone and killing more than half of them, had a record of only a fraction of that figure in Africa. As a result of these observations Dr. Burkitt first raised the question: What is it that seems to protect the Africans from such diseases?

Several other investigators have since taken up this hypothesis and designed studies to test it. Results of the studies vary, according to G. Spiller and H. Freeman in a 1981 article in the *American Journal of Clinical Nutrition*, but most investigators agree that dietary fiber has emerged in the past decade as an important factor in nutrition and medicine and appears to have complex and far-reaching effects on the physiology and health of man.

WHAT IS FIBER?

Many people are familiar with fiber but are not aware of what it does. In simple terms, fiber holds water, and thus provides bulk that moves food easily and quickly through the digestive tract, keeping the passages open. Fiber, particularly in the case of wheat fiber, is the part of the food that you don't digest; you eat it and you eliminate it.

In medical terms, fiber is a subclass of carbohydrates that consists of nonstarch polysaccharides and lignin, and its major constituents are cellulose, hemicellulose, lignin, and pectins, which are not broken down during passage through the gastrointestinal tract and are excreted in the stool.

FIBER IS AN ESSENTIAL NUTRIENT

Although fiber itself does not supply nutrients per se, fiber has now moved to the position of being an essential nutrient, the deficiency of which seems to have serious consequences. The fact is becoming more widely established that fiber does play an important role in metabolic functions and in the mechanical movement of stool.

According to Dr. Burkitt, the person most responsible for identifying the importance of fiber in the diet, the amount of fiber in the diet has a direct effect on the transit time of food. The transit time, the amount of time between when food is eaten and when it is eliminated, is a factor that is important in the usefulness of fiber. Dr. Burkitt observed the rarity of large-bowel cancer, for example, in most Africans, and suggested that populations consuming a diet rich in fiber have a lower incidence of this type of cancer, while those eating refined carbohydrates and little fiber had a higher incidence. Rural Africans, for example, had a fiber intake of 25 grams a day versus only a 6.4-gram daily intake in the United States. His research, reported in *Clinical Gastroenterology* in 1985, supported the fact that large-bowel tumors are related to factors characteristic of modern western society, where the transit time of food is longer; as a result, small, firm stools are produced. Dr. Burkitt went on to argue that slower transit time allows more time for gut bacteria to degrade intraluminal components, produce carcinogens (cancer-inducing products), and enable such carcinogens to act. Dr. Burkitt cited further studies that have shown that nearly all patients with constipation are helped by a liberal intake of fiber-rich foods, and, as a result, faster transit time of food. Dr. Burkitt pointed once again to the major difference between the African diet and the western diet.

The shorter transit time of food, as put forth by Dr. Burkitt in the *American Journal of Gastroenterology* has been suggested as having several benefits:

1. It reduces straining of muscles to move waste products along the intestine.
2. It helps protect against toxic materials in the intestine because it reduces the time undigested waste material and carcinogens spend in contact with the intestinal lining.
3. It lessens the pressure on blood vessels in the intestinal area as well as in the leg veins because of the ease of movement.
4. It decreases the reabsorption of bile salts with a resultant decrease in blood cholesterol.

Not all the investigators of transit time with fiber found it as useful in prevention and treatment of disease as did Dr. Burkitt. M. J. Hill in *Lancet*, for one, argued against it being involved and pointed to two epidemiological studies in which transit time had been measured in populations with widely differing large-bowel cancer risks, and no significant differences in transit time had been found. However, even this investigator did state that it was unwise to dismiss the transit-time benefit of fiber as being unimportant, since there did appear to be a measure of evidence that transit speed was indeed a determining factor, especially in colonic disease.

MORE GOOD NEWS ABOUT DIETARY FIBER

Dietary fiber can help lower blood pressure and cholesterol level, thus cutting the risk of heart attack; fiber can prevent and/or treat a number of intestinal disorders; fiber can prevent and/or treat hypoglycemia and diabetes; and fiber can help one lose weight as well. Studies show that a high-fiber diet can be useful in the prevention of some cancers such as cancer of the colon, prostate, breast, and ovary. The most recent evidence shows that fiber is being prescribed for a heart-healthy diet. Bypass-surgery patients are instructed to cut down on fat and to include more fiber in their diet. Fiber has been found to be useful in dealing with depression, varicose veins, gallstones, and irritable-bowel syndrome or recurring stomachache in children. And here's important news for those of us with high-speed life-styles: Fiber has been credited with providing a longer level of high energy because of its ability to smooth out the absorption time of food, thereby distributing energy to the body over a longer period of time instead of one blast of food or sugar energy.

According to Peter Greenwald, M.D., Director of Cancer Prevention and Control at the National Cancer Institute, there is evidence that fiber plays a protective role against cancer and is useful in the prevention of other diseases such as cardiovascular disease, diabetes, appendicitis, high blood pressure, and high blood cholesterol. He goes on to state that good advice to everyone who eats a typical American diet would be: Double your intake of dietary fiber.

THE EFFECTS OF BRAN FIBER

The healthful properties of fiber have been known for years; unfortunately, the average dietary intake of bran has shrunk to barely thirty percent of the necessary thirty to forty grams, or two to three heaped tablespoons, per day. This situation is attributed to highly processed foods, increased use of prepared foods, and greater carbohydrate consumption. Bran is a palatable, wholesome, and inexpensive source of dietary fiber that can be added to the everyday diet to bring the fiber content up to the required standards for good health.

♘ 2 ♘

Fiber Stands Guard Against Disease

THE MEDICAL INDICATIONS FOR BRAN FIBER

Fiber has been found not only to help guard against a variety of serious diseases but also to help treat many health problems. Primarily, fiber's beneficial role is related to its ability to contribute to gastrointestinal health. According to an article in *Progress in Food Nutritional Science*, the effects of bran are observable at all stages, from ingestion through elimination.

Following is a discussion of the different diseases that can be prevented and/or treated with the addition of dietary fiber. The scope of the list gives a clear indication of how crucial bran is in promoting good health.

Coronary Artery Disease (Heart Disease) This problem is responsible for one third of all deaths in the United States. Coronary heart disease is a disease of the arteries that supply blood to the heart muscle. The arteries can become lined with deposits that narrow the passages through which the blood flows.

The diseased arteries, choked with deposits, can prevent the heart from receiving the amount of blood it needs to work properly. It is this condition of blocked arteries that can cut off the blood supply to the heart, causing the death of the heart muscles. Even a partial restriction of the blood supply to the heart muscles can cause heart failure or severe pain.

Dietary fiber has been found to be useful in helping to keep the coronary arteries clear of such deposits. Much attention has been paid to the role of cholesterol in connection with heart problems because it is a major component of the arterial plaque that narrows artery walls. Recent research has shown that high fiber intake can play an important part in the prevention of coronary heart disease by cutting down on the amount of cholesterol that is circulating in the blood so that less is deposited on the arterial walls. In the article "Nutrition for the Older Adult" in *Occupational Health Nursing*, Maria Salerno pointed out that fiber-rich foods actually decrease the absorption of cholesterol and saturated fats from the gastrointestinal tract and increase their excretion from the body. She went on to say that many elderly persons believe that blood cholesterol levels can be controlled by simply limiting the number of eggs they consume. However, cholesterol is found in all animal food products, not just in eggs, as many believe. In addition, diets with an excess of saturated fats, sugar, and calories and inadequate fiber contribute to increased blood levels of cholesterol.

A second source of cholesterol has been shown to be the body itself. Researchers have pointed out that the human liver synthesizes cholesterol in large amounts, thereby further complicating the cholesterol problem, and that a fiber-rich diet has been found to increase the amount of cholesterol that is excreted in the daily bowel movement at the same time it reduces the amount of cholesterol secreted by the liver.

Another cause of heart attack is the blockage of the blood supply to the heart by a blood clot that has formed in the artery or lodged in a narrow portion of the artery. Research has suggested that fiber, particularly wheat bran, plays an important role in preventing the formation of blood clots in the bloodstream as well as in decreasing cholesterol deposits. The latter is particularly affected by oat bran. This last discussion points out the true value of increasing the bodily intake of both oat and wheat bran.

Research has also examined the effects of fats in connection with heart disease, especially animal fats. In 1972, H. Trowell and D. Burkitt observed and reported in *Advances in Lipid Research* that there was a decline in coronary heart disease rates during the period of World War II when a more crude wheat-flour preparation was taking place in England. Likewise, Dr. Burkitt as well as other researchers have reported that low-fiber diets often accompany coronary heart disease. The incidence of coronary heart disease was much lower in native African populations, where the intake of dietary fiber was much higher, even though this type of diet was also high in fats, especially animal fats.

Hypertension (High Blood Pressure) This health problem is most commonly found among middle-aged and older people but has been found increasingly in a wider range of people as a result of excessive salt consumption, obesity, and pregnancy. Hypertension is one of the risk factors in some types of heart disease and is once again found predominantly in westernized peoples. According to R. E. Hodges and T. Rebello in the article "Dietary Changes and Their Possible Effect on Blood Pressure" published in the *American Journal of Clinical Nutrition* in 1985, there is some evidence that the changes that occurred in the American diet in the years between 1941 and 1944, such as greater refinement of grain products and increased fat in the diet may well have encouraged the genesis of a portion of the high blood pressure and coronary heart disease that occurred in the United States. They further reported that it can be suggested that had the American servicemen been given more cereal food products, including high-fiber bread instead of excessive amounts of meat and fats, the dietary pattern of America might well have been substantially different. It was concluded that more study is needed to confirm or refute this hypothesis, but the likelihood of correlation between dietary habits and fiber and high blood pressure was good.

Experiments at Southampton University have shown that students with a high-fiber intake had lower blood pressure than those with a low-fiber intake. This study, published in the *British Medical Bulletin*, went on to point out that when those on a low fiber diet switched to a high-fiber intake, their blood pressure showed marked decreases within four weeks. The same effect was seen with regard to salt intake, the reduction of which helped lower high blood pressure.

Colon Cancer Colon cancer is the most frequent cross-gender cancer today. This malignancy is believed to be the result of carcinogens in the contents of the bowel. Like other digestive-tract problems, cancer of the colon has been linked directly to diet, and there has been significant evidence that the high intake of bran on a daily basis can help to prevent colon cancer.

In the *British Journal of Cancer*, B. S. Drasar and D. Irving reported a comparison of dietary data from the Food and Agriculture Organization and colon-cancer data from thirty-seven countries which showed that the incidence of colon cancer was directly related to the intake of animal protein and fat. Excess fat in the diet along with inadequate fiber intake has been shown to result in increased carcinogens in the bowel.

The relationship of dietary fiber to colon cancer also revolves around the interactions of dietary fiber in bile-acid metabolism. Fats in the colon increase the amount of bile salts, which bacteria may convert into carcinogens. Bile acids act as promoters of colon cancer. Epidemiological evidence links the concentrations of fecal bile acids with colon cancer both in populations with higher risk of colon cancer and in patients with colon cancer.

Fiber moves the waste material and harmful substances through the intestine more quickly so that there is less time for carcinogens and other poisonous substances in the waste mass to be in contact with the intestinal lining. Further, fiber provides a bulking material that absorbs water, which is believed to dilute any carcinogens that are present in the digestive tract. According to B. S. Reddy in the article "Dietary Fibre and Colon Cancer: Epidemiologic and Experimental Evidence," published in the *Canadian Medical Association Journal*, the protective effect of dietary fiber may be due to adsorption or dilution of carcinogens by the components of the fiber.

Whatever the case, Reddy pointed out that dietary fiber could affect the enterohepatic circulation of bile salts, thereby reducing the formation of potential tumor promoters in the colon and, as a result, be useful in the prevention of various intestinal diseases, especially colon cancer. J. H. Cummings et al. pointed out in an article published in the *American Journal of Clinical Nutrition* in 1976 that the effect of fiber on the colon is due to both its physical and its chemical properties and varies with the individual, the type of fiber, and the amount ingested.

Dr. Burkitt reported that there are strong indications that increased fiber intake protects against large-bowel cancers by increasing fecal bulk, which speeds intestinal passage of stool. Dr. Burkitt pointed again to the low incidence of colon cancer in the people of Africa and Asia, who eat diets that are low in animal fat and high in fiber, as evidence in favor of fiber as protection against cancer.

Breast Cancer Breast cancer is a serious and growing health problem that has recently been linked with diet. Medical research material has suggested that women's breasts take up toxic waste products that have been reabsorbed into the bloodstream from waste material that lingers in the large intestine. The increased transit speed in waste products provided by dietary fiber has been reported to be a possible help in the prevention of breast cancer. Associations have been noted between constipation and lumpy breasts, chronic cystic disease, and cancer. Cystic disease has been seen to improve when constipation is relieved. Lumpy breasts can be caused by changes in hormone balance that can be brought about through changes in the levels of fat in the diet. Most recently, the September 1988 article by P. Goodwin published in the *British Journal of Surgery* seems to confirm the relationship between lumpy painful breasts and blood fats. It has been further suggested by Maria Salerno that women with painful breast swelling have found some relief on a high-fiber diet. According to a study by N. Fisher et al. reported in the *American Journal of Clinical Nutrition* in 1985, there were significantly fewer mammary tumors found in a lifespan study on rats on high-fiber diets than in those fed the low-fiber diets.

Ovarian and Prostate Cancer As with breast cancer, increased transit time of fiber has been suggested as being useful in the prevention of ovarian and prostate cancer. Bran provides the bulk for rapid transit of dietary fat and a prevention of the formation of cancer-causing substances. Ovarian cancer and prostate cancer are both hormone-dependent health problems; however, research reported by M. J. Hill in the article "Dietary Fat and Human Cancer" in the *Proceedings of the Nutrition Society* in 1981 has found a strong correlation between dietary fat and the mortality of these two types of cancer.

Diverticulosis This is one of the most painful health problems as well as the most common of the large intestine or colon, to the extent that one-half of all older Americans are victims of it. Diverticular disease is a condition in which pockets, or pouches, are formed in the wall of the large intestine. Pressure on the intestinal walls by constipation or hard stools can cause severe abdominal pain as well as nausea, vomiting, distention, chills, and/or fever. At one time patients with diverticular disease were placed on low-fiber diets, which were supposed to be useful in avoiding any irritating roughage. Now it is recognized that dietary fiber is not rough or irritating; rather, fiber provides the means with which to move waste material quickly and easily through the intestine. One interesting study in particular was done by J. Weinreich in London, in which he compared a high-wheat-bran-fiber diet and a low-fiber diet in 105 patients suffering from symptomatic diverticular disease. Data collected after three, six, and twelve months showed that the group on bran had the greatest improvement. The conclusion was that there was evidence showing that a low-fiber diet might lead to the further development of diverticular disease and that patients with the disease are relieved by a higher fiber content in their diet.

Dr. Neil Painter, a London surgeon, reported that the complete reversal of earlier approaches has resulted in diverticular disease of the colon being better managed by the use of high-fiber diets, and that colon surgery has frequently been avoided altogether. Available information has indicated that the incidence of diverticular disease is low in populations ingesting large amounts of fiber, and there is now general clinical consensus that a high-fiber diet is the treatment of choice in uncomplicated diverticular disease. The *American Journal of Clinical Nutrition* supported the theory that a high-fiber diet may prevent diverticulosis as well as relieve the symptoms of the disease once it has set in.

Diabetes This health problem occurs when there is a lack of effective insulin to make energy available to the body through the correct use of blood sugar. Insulin is a hormone produced in the pancreas and is responsible for dealing with sugar once it has been absorbed into the blood from the intestine. It is the job of insulin to make energy available to the body. Without enough insulin, sugar will build up in the blood and starve the body of energy. The sugar is then excreted in the urine rather than used by the body. Many recent reports have suggested that a high-fiber diet can improve control of diabetes and be useful in diabetic therapy. In 1986, Drs. Anderson and Gustafson of the University of Kentucky and the Endocrine-Metabolic Section of the Veterans Administration Medical Center in Lexington reported that a high-fiber diet helps reduce the need for insulin to the extent that high-fiber diets eliminated the need for insulin injections for two-thirds of patients who developed diabetes in later years. They went on to report that a high-fiber diet cut back by twenty-five percent the amount of insulin needed by diabetics whose diabetes began in childhood. The doctors also pointed out that bran lowered blood fat and cholesterol, significant to the diabetic since heart attack is the cause of more than one half of diabetes-related deaths.

Improvements in diabetic control and reduction in insulin and drug requirements have been reported in both mild and moderate diabetics on high-fiber diets. For example, in Britain, white and black mildly hypertensive Type 2 diabetics were given a diet high in fiber while low in fat for a period of three months and the results were reported in the *Diabetes Resident*. Both white and black diabetic patient groups demonstrated a significantly improved condition, which would suggest that dietary fiber might be considered an attractive alternative to conventional antihypertensive drug therapy in mildly hypertensive Type 2 diabetic black as well as white patients. Further studies like the one reported in the *Annals of Internal Medicine* have reported that high-fiber diets for diabetics have resulted in some patients getting along with oral antidiabetes drugs and allowing other patients to reduce insulin dosage. Benefits of improved glycemic control and lowered blood lipids continue as patients follow high-fiber, high-carbohydrate diets over time. Drs. Anderson and Gustafson furthermore reported in *Geriatrics* that in their experience, high-fiber diets produced good health results in diabetics for up to ten years of follow-up. They pointed out that in addition to minimizing the need for drugs, the high-fiber diet was well tolerated by diabetic patients and their family members. The high-fiber diet for the diabetic is, in fact, recommended to the entire family by the American Heart Association and the National Cancer Institute.

Hypoglycemia (Low Blood Sugar) This is a health problem that can be another result of eating too many low-fiber foods, and, as with diabetes, a suggested treatment has been dietary fiber. Bran has been reported to protect against problems of hypoglycemia and hyperglycemia by modulating glucose absorption from the gastrointestinal tract. Fiber has been found to provide a steady stream of fuel for the body that does not make undue demands on insulin production.

Obesity (Weight Gain/Loss) Overweight and obesity are common in western society, and as a result, weight loss is often recommended to reduce the morbidity and mortality associated with those conditions. In 1986, it was estimated by the *American Journal of Public Health* that over twenty-five percent of the American public is seriously overweight and that over forty percent of the European population is trying to lose weight at any one time. B. R. Bistrian reported in the *Archives of Internal Medicine* that low-fat/high-fiber diets are particularly effective for weight loss, and that they are also associated with changes in blood lipids that might be beneficial with regard to the risk of cardiovascular disease as well as obesity.

Evidence to substantiate the fact that fiber can help promote healthy weight loss was reported on a personal basis by Dr. K. W. Heaton of the University of Bristol, in the *British Medical Journal*. Dr. Heaton noticed some years ago that when he and his wife increased fiber in their diets, they lost weight. This was not a dramatic loss, but a slow one that began by simply substituting high-fiber whole wheat bread for refined white bread. In 1981, Dr. Heaton encouraged colleagues to do the same and documented on an informal basis that their weight losses, while using bran and changing nothing else about their regular diets over several months, went as high as fifteen pounds.

A more formal study was done in 1986 at Oxford, England, in which 135 overweight subjects were recruited to test the difference between a low-carbohydrate diet and a low-fat/high-fiber diet. The two diet groups appeared evenly balanced with regard to weight and other factors. The participants ranged from barely overweight to obese, and there were more females than males. Over ninety-five percent participated fully in the one- and the three-month follow-up sessions, and eighty-eight percent took part in the one-year measurements. One of the strengths of this study was the real-life setting, in contrast with most metabolic studies. The conclusion was that there was measurable effectiveness with the low-fat/high-fiber diet group, which had greater weight loss, a lowering of total cholesterol, and a willingness to continue with the diet. There is evidence that fiber decreases the number of calories that the body absorbs from food. Because fiber speeds up the elimination of digested foods, fat and protein may be excreted instead of absorbed and stored as excess fat. As H. Trowell and Dr. Burkitt had reported in the article "The Physiological Role of Dietary Fiber: A Ten-Year Review," out of a typical modern diet, 93.2 percent of the available calories in the food can be absorbed. With the addition of fiber as whole wheat bread included in the diet, the figure decreases to eighty-eight percent because of the increased transit speed. Along with decreased calorie absorption, Maria Salerno pointed out that fiber has a slowing effect on digestion, therefore supplying energy for a longer period of time; that fiber, which takes longer to eat, will satisfy oral cravings more completely than refined foods; and that because fiber attracts water and swells up in the digestive tract, it gives the subject a sense of appetite satisfaction for greater periods of time. It has also been reported that fiber in the diet can take the place of some fat intake.

Constipation This is a common condition due to the failure of the bowel to eliminate waste products thoroughly and easily. This condition is characterized by infrequent bowel movements or the passage of hard, dry stools. Without the benefit of the fluid-retaining activity of fiber, stools tend to be small in volume and hard, thus slow-moving. Constipation can be caused by lack of exercise, by some drugs, by stress, by poor diet, by insufficient fiber in the diet, or any combination of these. Habitual use of laxatives can result in a bowel that is unable to function on its own. Furthermore, daily use of laxatives could result in the loss of necessary body salt.

Physical straining that can occur in constipation can result in more serious diseases such as hiatal hernia, varicose veins, and hemorrhoids. Constipation is often associated with diverticular disease, especially with people over the age of fifty. According to Dr. Burkitt, it is the decreased transit time, the interval between when a meal is eaten and when the remains are eliminated, provided by the fiber that can help prevent constipation and its related disorders. Through his research Dr. Burkitt estimated that an African diet of high-fiber natural foods passed through the system in about one and one-half days. The transit time of a western diet was between two and three days in a young, healthy person and up to two weeks in an elderly person.

The proposed protective effect of increased stool weight has been tested epidemiologically by measuring fecal output in populations with high and low cancer risk. The studies show that the highest stool weights were in those populations with the lowest cancer risk. For example, the stools of native Africans have been found to weigh as much as 500 grams a day compared with the 100-gram average in constipated westerners, according to Dr. Burkitt. An increase in fecal output is an almost invariable response to an increased intake of dietary fiber. Several dietary experiments have confirmed this effect of fiber. In the study done in Oxford and reported in the *American Journal of Public Health*, 135 overweight subjects were recruited to test the difference of two diets, a low-carbohydrate diet and a low-fat/high-fiber diet. At the end of the three-month test period, it was noted that constipation was a more common complaint among the low-carbohydrate subjects, or twenty-three percent, versus three percent in the low-fat/high-fiber diet.

Irritable-Bowel Syndrome   This ailment is one of the most common of all digestive-system problems for both adults and children. The symptoms include abdominal pain, or stomachache, distention, constipation alternating with diarrhea, nausea, heartburn, and excessive belching. This syndrome is also known as irritable colon and spastic colon. Medical studies have indicated that a high-fiber diet will improve these digestive problems. Fiber has been found to help improve constipation as well as deal with diarrhea. At the Bristol Royal Infirmary in Bristol, England, patients with irritable-bowel syndrome took part in a controlled comparison trial of diets with high-fiber and low-fiber content. After six weeks the subjects on the high-fiber diet showed improvement in all irritable-bowel symptoms and in objective measurements of colon activity. There were no recorded improvements on the low-fiber diet. Likewise, A. P. Manning et al. reported in the article "Wheat Fiber and the Irritable-Bowel Syndrome," published in *Lancet*, that bran was used in the therapy of the irritable-bowel syndrome and that a subjective improvement had occurred with a reduction in colonic motor activity in subjects that were treated with fiber.

In children, it is the recurrent abdominal pain known as the stomachache that has presented numerous diagnostic problems for parents and pediatricians. Recurrent abdominal pain is reported to affect ten to eighteen percent of school-age children and is caused by obvious organic pathology in fewer than ten percent of cases. W. Feldman et al. did a random study with controlled trials of additional dietary fiber in fifty-two children with recurrent abdominal pain. The study showed a statistically significant decrease in pain attacks, at least fifty percent fewer attacks in the subjects given the added fiber. They pointed out that although the cause of recurrent abdominal pain is poorly understood, the study supported the hypothesis that the beneficial effect of added fiber appears to be due to its effect of shortening transit time. The *American Journal of Diseases of Children* has reported that the use of dietary fiber will reduce the incidence of recurrent stomachache in children.

Appendicitis Appendicitis is the most common abdominal surgical emergency in the United States. This health problem occurs in the intestine when a blind-ended tube about two inches in length becomes blocked and then infected. This condition is usually caused by a small lump of hard feces, the kind of waste material that is typical of a low-fiber diet. Bran, by absorbing water, produces soft waste material, which lessens the likelihood of a blockage by hard feces. Fiber also induces a shorter transit time for food, thus allowing less time for bowel bacteria to multiply in the appendix.

Appendicitis is a health problem rarely found among people of underdeveloped areas. At Baragwanath Hospital, located in Johannesburg, South Africa, appendicitis was observed in 3.6 percent of the black patients, and at the same time, in fifty to seventy-five percent of the white patients, according to I. Segal, A. Solomon, and J. A. Hunt in the article "Emergence of Diverticular Disease in the Urban South African Black." Furthermore, Segal et al. reported there are about two cases of appendicitis per thousand admissions of rural adults annually, a low frequency consistent with the tenfold differential of appendectomies reported to prevail in urban black and white adolescents. But like heart disease, this disease is something that people develop when they move to urbanized environments and change to western diets.

The *American Journal of Public Health* has recently reported that appendicitis occurs in children for the same reason as in adults. Children who eat small amounts of fiber are twice as likely to have appendicitis as children who have a high-fiber diet. This statistic was borne out at the University of Washington School of Public Health and Community Medicine in Seattle, where a study was done on 135 children with appendicitis and 212 comparison children with relation to their diet. It was found that children who had an intake of whole-grain foods were estimated to have a fifty percent lower risk of appendicitis.

Gallstones Almost entirely because of cholesterol gallstones, 500,000 gallbladders are surgically removed each year in the United States. Gallstones form in the gallbladder when there is an excess of cholesterol in the bile. After food is eaten, the gallbladder excretes bile, which contains substances necessary to digest fatty foods. Bile consists of cholesterol and bile salts, and stones are formed when the excess cholesterol is deposited as stones. Research on both humans and animals has suggested that fiber can help reduce stone formation. According to an article published in *Advances in Lipid Research*, dietary fiber, or more specifically wheat bran, had been shown to reduce deoxycholate levels in the bile-salt pool, a change that had resulted in reduced biliary cholesterol levels and therefore reduced stones. It was similarly reported that by feeding bran for four to six weeks to a group of ten women with probable cholesterol gallstones, there was a fifteen percent reduction in the cholesterol in the bile of the subjects.

Fiber has also been found to bind and increase the excretion of bile salts and prevent them from getting back into the system. Before using bran, nine of the ten patients had supersaturated bile, while after bran feeding, seven of the ten displayed reduced saturation of bile. These data indicated a change in total bile-acid-pool size, which in turn would result in less cholesterol deposit as stones. Dr. Burkitt had hypothesized that fiber-depleted diets predispose to overnutrition (overeating), and this in turn increases cholesterol in bile. It is widely accepted, according to Dr. Burkitt, that the consumption of refined-carbohydrate foods and lack of fiber contributes to the production of supersaturated bile, and, as a result, it has been argued that this indicates that gallstones are a largely preventable condition.

Hemorrhoids (Piles)   This condition has been described as enlarged veins in the mucous membrane inside or just outside the rectum, or a prolapse of the part of the anal region that contains blood vessels. Hemorrhoids are an extremely common affliction according to Z. Cohen, who reported in the *Canadian Journal of Surgery* that the prevalence of hemorrhoids ranges from one in twenty-five to one in thirty individuals in North America. This health problem has been attributed to the straining and stress caused when passing hard stools. Other factors that may contribute to the problem are heredity and prolonged standing. Hemorrhoids may produce bleeding from the rectum and often make elimination painful. Many British surgeons routinely prescribe fiber-rich diets for all patients with hemorrhoids and bleeding hemorrhoids before trying other treatment. Likewise, in

Holland, patients with hemorrhoids no longer are referred initially to surgeons, but to gastroenterologists, who prescribe high-fiber diets after excluding other serious causes of bleeding. In one study in Sweden, nineteen outpatients with a history of hemorrhoids were given a six-week treatment of bran fiber in their daily diet. In all cases, a normalization of transit time occurred with the use of the fiber, relieving the painful symptoms of hemorrhoids, thereby further supporting the hypothesis that dietary fiber is useful in the treatment of hemorrhoids. In the *South African Medical Journal,* A. R. Walker, like other researchers, has suggested that diet clearly has been implicated in the predisposition to constipation, hemorrhoids, and diverticular disease.

Hiatal Hernia Often there are no symptoms of this abnormal upward protrusion of the top of the stomach into the chest cavity through the opening in the diaphragm. In some cases, however, the protrusion causes a return flow of juices from the stomach into the esophagus, and such symptoms as heartburn and burning pain behind the breastbone. Hiatus hernias are believed to be the direct result of straining during elimination. This condition has become prevalent in middle-aged people who eat a low-fiber diet. Hiatus hernia has its maximum prevalence in economically developed communities in North America and western Europe. Dr. Burkitt has reported on a large series of upper gastrointestinal tract radiologic examinations which indicate that this defect has been demonstrated in over twenty percent of North American adults. In contrast, he goes on to cite research that showed that the disease is rare in situations typified by rural African communities. In Kenya, for instance, only one case had been found in over one thousand examinations, and in Tanzania, one in over seven hundred examinations. Dr. Burkitt's article "Hiatus Hernia: Is It Preventable?" concluded that fiber-depleted diets are a major factor in the causation of hiatus hernia, which is consistent with all that is known of the disease.

Varicose Veins More than ten percent of all Americans have varicose veins. This condition is closely related to the health problem of constipation and is often mentioned in the same literature, even though very little research has been directed at varicose veins and fiber specifically. The available literature has suggested that it is the straining caused by constipation that can cause blood to be forced to flow back down the legs, causing the valves to stretch. Eventually, the veins will not be able to function properly, and varicose veins will develop. In a 1972 *Lancet* publication, Dr. Burkitt suggested fiber as a treatment for varicose veins, because it had been found to deal successfully with the condition of constipation. Therefore, he proposed that fiber could be useful as a means of preventing further damage to veins from occurring, and most important, to reduce the chances of the complications of varicose veins, which can be phlebothrombosis, thrombophlebitis (phlebitis), and pulmonary embolism. Hereditary disposition to varicose veins can make one more susceptible to the condition, but research has found that ease in bowel movements, which will mean less strain and pressure on the blood vessels, could lessen certain ailments such as varicose veins.

Depression and Irritability   This common health problem has just recently been linked with fiber. A study by David Levitsky, Ph.D., of the Committee on Nutrition in Medical Education, suggested that high fiber intake may have a reversing effect on depression and irritability. Dr. Levitsky pointed out that when the intestinal tract is full, amino acids, which promote satisfaction, are released; this in turn lessens both depression and irritability. This fact could prove to be useful to dieters, for, as Dr. Levitsky goes on to report, the satisfaction of fullness could take place with fiber without the calorie intake.

Protection Against Food Additives   The possibility that fiber could provide some protection against potentially toxic effects of food additives and drugs has been raised by Dr. B. H. Ershoff of Loma Linda University in 1985, and reported on by the Committee on Nutrition in Medical Education. High levels of the sweetener cyclamate were fed to rats, some on high-fiber and some on low-fiber diets. The same procedure was followed with various drugs, chemicals, and food additives, using both rats and mice as subjects. All the studies indicated that the materials were poisonous to rats and mice on low-fiber diets but had no deleterious effects when fed with diets high in fiber. The studies suggested that it was the decreased transit time provided by the fiber bulk that moved the potentially poisonous materials through the system more quickly, allowing for less possibility of contamination.

WHAT IS THE RATIONALE FOR THE USE OF BRAN?

The McGovern report on Dietary Goals for the United States, published in 1977, suggested seven changes in food selection and preparation. Heading the list as reported in the *Journal of Human Nutrition* was this suggestion: Increase consumption of whole-grain fiber.

Dietary guidelines published in Australia, Norway, and Sweden have similarly encouraged increased fiber in the diet, and the Centre of Agricultural Strategy in the United Kingdom has suggested further that health may benefit by increased bran consumption. It appears that enough evidence has been accumulated to suggest that a significant role is played by dietary fiber.

Even though there are controversies that remain to be further explored, clinicians and scientists agree that there is a definite niche for fiber in medicine and nutrition, according to G. Spiller and H. Freeman in a 1981 article "Recent Advances in Dietary Fiber and Colorectal Diseases" that appeared in the *American Journal of Clinical Nutrition*. Spiller went on to point out that contrary to popular belief, it is not necessary to eat pounds of bran daily. Indications are that as little as two or three tablespoons per day of combined oat and wheat brans is usually enough to take advantage of the substantial benefits that bran has to offer.

❧ 3 ❧

The Different Types of Bran Fiber

WHAT YOU SHOULD KNOW ABOUT THE KINDS OF BRAN FIBER

The kind of fiber in the diet has also become a matter of investigation, since the strength of protection varies with the type of fiber. The isolation and study of individual fibers have represented the most systematic approach to defining the effects of different chemical types of fiber. Many types of dietary fiber are substantially digested in the large bowel and thus provide an opportunity for microbial growth. For this reason, researchers have suggested that less digestible materials such as bran are the most useful to the digestive system. The authors have concluded that the effect a particular fiber has on colonic function depends on its physical and chemical composition and thus its digestibility. They demonstrated this point with a test in which vegetable and fruit fiber was used on one group of subjects while bran fiber was used on a second group. It was reported by B. S. Reddy in the *Canadian Medical Association Journal* that the fecal weight of the second group was increased by 127 percent when bran was added to the diet, while in the first group the fecal weight was increased by only twenty percent when carrots, cabbage, and apples were added. R. M. Kay and A. S. Truswell in an article in the *British Journal of Nutrition* likewise showed that by adding wheat fiber to the diet, the transit time was shortened and the concentration of fecal bile acids was decreased, as opposed to the addition of natural fiber (vegetables and fruits), where the added pectin to the diet showed a measurably smaller difference to both the transit time and the lessening of bile acids.

To further prove this point, a test in Britain was conducted with a mixed diet of fiber sources, including cereals and fruits and vegetables, which resulted in an average overall digestibility of eighty percent, while a diet of bran had a digestibility of fifty-eight percent, adding support to the theory that bran fiber is the least digestible type of fiber and therefore the most useful to the elimination process. J. A. Ritchie et al reported in *Gut* on studies that showed that wheat bran had the most measurable effect on the concentration of bile acids in the stool of any tested fiber. They also pointed out that wheat bran had a greater capacity as a vehicle for water and therefore was useful in eliminating constipation as well as diarrhea at the same time it increased the rate of transit and stool bulk.

SOURCES OF FIBER

The progress in understanding fiber has been slow because it is a difficult material to handle from the standpoint of the laboratory; its action depends on both its physical and chemical properties, and few people have expertise in both areas and, too, ade-

methods for its measurement are still being developed.

Fiber has become an important component of the diet and has been shown by recent research to have physiological effects on health; however, it is not a single substance. The studies on fiber have demonstrated that different types of fiber act in different ways depending on their source; for example, as reported by A. M. Stephan in the *Journal of Human Nutrition*, vegetable fiber and cereal fiber have been found to be quite different in chemical properties.

There are two main classes of fiber, insoluble and soluble:

1. Insoluble fiber cannot be dissolved in water, is primarily in a whole-grain product such as wheat bran.
2. Soluble fiber dissolves in water, is found in fruits, vegetables, barley, and oats.

Each form of fiber has been found to have a particular function in the body. The six most important types of dietery fiber are:

Insoluble:
1. Lignin—an inert woody substance that is more resistant to digestion than other fibers.
2. Cellulose—the main structural component of the plant cell walls and the most abundant molecule in nature.
3. Hemicellulose—smaller than cellulose and more accessible to bacterial enzymes.

Soluble:
4. Gums—the sticky excretions of the plant cell walls.
5. Pectins—found in vegetables and fruits; also from gels and used in making jams and jellies.

6. Mucilages—the secretions in plant seeds that prevent dehydration of the seed.

While wheat bran is totally an insoluble fiber, insoluble fiber is also found in oat bran, corn bran, and cereal grains. It has been found to absorb water and add bulk to soften the stool, thereby increasing transit speed of fecal material. Soluble fiber is found principally in fruits, vegetables, beans, oats, and nuts. It has been found to be useful in controlling blood cholesterol and glucose levels, and in affecting the absorption of sugar and fats. Most plant foods have been found to contain both soluble and insoluble fiber; however, the amount and type may vary from food to food. It is the cellular structure of bran fiber that makes it so useful to the digestive system.

WHAT KINDS OF BRAN FIBER ARE USEFUL TO GOOD HEALTH?

There are three main types of bran fiber that aid in digestion and in the elimination process.

1. Wheat bran—considered to be a pure source of fiber, is the least digestible of all the fiber sources, and therefore the most useful in increasing the transit speed of food. Wheat bran also has the most measurable effect on the concentration of bile acids, that is, it does the most to decrease bile acids, which can become cancer-producing products in the intestinal tract.
2. Oat bran—more readily digested than wheat bran, which results in a slower transit time. Oat bran has been found to be useful in lowering blood cholesterol levels as well as in regulating the body's use of sugar.
3. Corn bran—has only one-third insoluble fiber of

wheat bran, and as a result is more readily digested than wheat bran.

Oat bran, a fermentable product like fruits and vegetables, is soluble fiber that binds on to bile acids made of cholesterol, which are then excreted. Wheat bran is insoluble, does not ferment in the body as fruits and vegetables do, and binds on to cancer-causing products as well as bile acids while moving through the body quickly.

❧ 4 ❧

Why You Need Both Oat Bran and Wheat Bran in Your Diet

THE STARTLING MEDICAL EVIDENCE

Because of their different content of soluble fibers, both oat bran and wheat bran are necessary to your everyday diet. They make very significant different contributions to your overall health, therefore one kind of fiber alone, such as oat bran, is not sufficient to provide a bran-fiber-full-health diet. Even more significant is the latest evidence that soluble or fermentable fibers such as oat bran have the potential to lead to tumor or cancer development.

As you know, oat bran, a fermentable product, is soluble fiber that binds on to bile acids made of cholesterol, which are then excreted. Oat bran is absorbed by the body, and as a result, the "good" cholesterol (high-density lipoprotein—HDL) helps sweep the "bad" cholesterol (low-density lipoprotein—LDL) from the veins and arteries. Wheat bran, on the other hand, is water insoluble, not absorbed by the body, and as a result moves through the body rapidly, taking carcinogens with it.

Of the various types of bran, wheat bran, which has no calories, has been found to be the least digestible fiber of all the fiber sources and is therefore the most effective in increasing transit speed in the intestinal tract. This was pointed out in a 1981 test by J. H. Cummings, comparing wheat bran and corn bran, in which the bran particles, or lignin, were clearly recognizable in feces recovered by subjects taking extra bran in their diets as opposed to other fibers. Wheat bran particles were most frequently identified at the end of the study, whereas the corn bran, which had only one-third the lignin content of the wheat bran, was seldom found.

In a study by A. J. M. Brodribb and C. Groves, reported in *Gut*, twenty-one volunteers were given twenty grams of coarse wheat bran for a week, and the next week this group was given twenty grams of oat bran. The results of the collected fecal samples showed that the particle size of the wheat bran was one-third larger than that of the oat bran. The oat bran, which proved to be highly water soluble, was more readily digested than the wheat bran; however, oat bran has been reported by J. W. Anderson and N. J. Gustafson in the article "Type II Diabetes: Current Nutrition Management Concepts" in *Geriatrics* to be useful in lowering blood cholesterol levels and in regulating the body's use of sugar.

According to N. S. Painter and Dr. Burkitt, wheat bran, because of its insolubility, has been repeatedly suggested for treatment of several intestinal diseases. Oat bran and corn bran have shown to be effective in adding needed fiber to the diet, and oat bran has the capacity to bind to cholesterol and eliminate it from the body.

However, the latest information on bran fiber suggests that oat bran could contribute to cancer. Important evidence reported in *Preventive Medicine* in July 1987 by L. R. Jacobs showed that because of their solubility, oat bran and corn bran may stimulate colon carcinogenesis by increasing fecal bile acid excretion, a feature of soluble fibers. Likewise, in the *Proceedings of the Society for Experimental Biology and Medicine* it was reported that a number of fermentable fiber supplements, including pectin, corn bran, oat bran, undegraded carageenan, agar, psyllium, guar gum, and alfalfa, have been shown to enhance tumor development. The article goes on to say that these stated fibers, when used in conjunction with wheat bran, which is insoluble, could prove to be useful fiber to the health of the body. The report concluded that more metabolic and physiological studies are needed to fully define the mechanisms by which certain fibers inhibit while others enhance colon carcinogenesis. In *Preventive Medicine* it was reported that fibers differ in their effect on stool bulk, with wheat fiber being a more effective stool-bulking agent than fruit and vegetable fibers; the researchers went on to state that wheat bran reduces fecal bile acid concentration whereas oat bran does not.

Once again it is the transit-time factor that is required for health benefits from the use of dietary fiber. In the July 1987 article "Starchy Foods, Type of Fiber, and Cancer Risk" in *Preventive Medicine* by D. J. Jenkins, it was pointed out that the soluble fibers (as oat bran or corn bran) have little effect on fecal bulk because they are largely fermented to short-chain fatty acids. The article goes on to state that insoluble fibers (as wheat bran) are much less fermented and therefore enhance fecal bulk, which increases the transit speed through the body.

The U.S. Department of Agriculture Dietary Guidelines have confirmed the need for Americans to increase their consumption of dietary bran. The average amount of dietary fiber intake is estimated to be at five to ten grams per person per day. The amount of dietary fiber intake should be thirty to forty grams per day. According to Dr. Burkitt in the article "Dietary Fibre, Is It Really Helpful?" the current average fiber intake could profitably be at least doubled, predominantly in the form of cereal fiber. Dr. Burkitt went on to specify that cereal fiber refers to bran fiber or the fiber from the grain kernel like oat bran and wheat bran as opposed to commercial cereals, which often include overprocessed grain with added sugar and salt. Therefore, using commercial fiber cereals such as a creamy-style oat bran cereal in cooking will double the amount of fat, sugar, and salt to the food while providing a minimal amount of bran fiber in your diet.

According to *Preventive Medicine*, recommendations to increase consumption of fiber-containing food and decrease the intake of dietary fat should form the basis of a diet that is unlikely to do harm and may have the potential for reducing the development of colon cancer in humans. Therefore, the need was suggested for the use of both oat bran and wheat bran. Furthermore, the article states that the feeding of wheat bran appears to inhibit colon-tumor development to a greater degree than do other dietary sources of fiber, even though other sources of fiber can be beneficial.

Research on the isolation and study of individual fibers suggests that wheat bran may be the therapy of choice in the successful long-term treatment of several intestinal diseases. Oat bran may be the bran of choice for lowering cholesterol levels in the blood. The accumulated evidence on fiber has indicated a need for increased consumption of the cereal fibers wheat bran and oat bran, because these fibers in particular when used together have been reported to be protective in relation to disease incidence.

BRAN FIBER VS. FIBER MEDICATION

Medical information concurs that it is best to increase fiber content in the diet by eating high-fiber food rather than using fiber medications, according to Maria Salerno. Primarily this is because some fiber medications or pills cannot be taken while taking other medications, such as tetracycline. Also, nutrition experts have cautioned against certain fiber medications because pure fiber in the form of pills, capsules, or powders can block the absorption of minerals such as calcium, iron, or zinc, while bran fiber eventually replaces the same nutrient that it initially blocks. Furthermore, fiber medications taken all at once in the amount that would satisfy a full health requirement could cause its own problems of constipation, cramps, distention, and excessive gas; whereas, with bran in food, the body is able to digest the food and the fiber together in a measured fashion, especially when the daily required amount of fiber is divided among two to three of the daily meals.

The overwhelming factor in bran fiber vs. fiber medication is the cost factor. The cost of adding bran in bulk to the diet is considerably less than the cost of purchasing fiber pills, capsules, wafers, or powders. And thus far, there has been no scientific evidence to show that fiber medications can achieve the full health or weight-reduction benefits of a high-fiber diet. Producers of fiber diet aids such as FiberCon by Lederle recommend that a person consume as many as eight to fifteen tablets a day to achieve the equivalent of thirty to forty grams of bran per day. This required amount is available in two to three tablespoons of bran per day at a fraction of the cost of fiber medications, while fiber aids in the form of wafers, pills, powders, or capsules would currently result in a cost from $10 to $15 per month for an adequate supply of fiber medication. According to Dr. David Reuben, the amount of bulk bran fiber that would be required for a full fiber diet could be averaged at less than one dollar per month, or about two cents per day.

❧ 5 ❧

How Much Bran Fiber Do You Need?

HOW TO INTRODUCE BRAN TO YOUR DAILY DIET

At present, there are no federal guidelines for the exact amount of fiber needed for good health. Contrary to popular belief, it is not necessary to eat pounds of bran fiber daily. Research shows that as little as two to three tablespoons (about thirty to forty grams) per day is usually enough to take advantage of the substantial health benefits bran has to offer.

Ideally, using both oat bran and wheat bran provides full health benefits. It is best to begin to use bran fiber slowly.

For adults:
1. Start with a teaspoon per day (about five grams).
2. Slowly increase the amount to two or three tablespoons per day (thirty to forty grams).
3. Implement this program over a ten- to sixteen-week period.

For children between five and twelve years of age:
1. Start with one-half teaspoon per day.
2. Slowly increase the amount to about one table-spoon per day.
3. Implement this program over a ten- to sixteen-week period.

For children between three and five years of age:
1. Needed daily amount is about one-half to one teaspoon.
2. Most young children will get the needed amount from a portion of the prepared family food.

Experts suggest that by gradually introducing bran into your diet and your metabolic system, you will have fewer problems with bloating, gas, or poor absorption of vitamins and minerals. Experts also suggest that fresh fruits and vegetables be included in the diet along with the bran. These give added water to body functions and help increase transit speed as well.

The average American diet consists of about five to ten grams of bran daily. Five grams of bran are about half an ounce, or roughly one teaspoon. Indications are that two to three tablespoons per day is enough to provide full health benefits from bran fiber.

This amount of bran fiber can be taken in three ways:

1. Put two to three tablespoons of bran fiber in a glass of water, mix as well as possible, and drink.
2. Include fiber in everyday food. This way it is possible to introduce your system and your taste buds gradually to bran fiber by disguising the bran fiber in the foods that you already enjoy. You can easily turn low-fiber foods into high-fiber foods.
3. Take fiber medication pills or powders. This is

expensive, promotes pill-taking, cannot be taken with certain medicines, and may block the absorption of certain minerals.

WHAT ARE THE PRECAUTIONS WITH THE USE OF BRAN FIBER?

As with any dietary component, intake of dietary fiber must be kept moderate at the onset to avoid possible ill effects of overconsumption. Research has suggested that bran fiber be introduced to the diet with one teaspoon of bran per day, gradually increasing the amount of bran fiber to two to three tablespoons per day. This should be done over a ten- to sixteen-week period, according to Dr. Burkitt in the *American Journal of Clinical Nutrition*. Most investigators of fiber have suggested that the change to a high-fiber diet should be a gradual one, and one that has a combination of bran and natural fibers such as fruits and vegetables.

The most important precaution is to increase water intake with the use of bran fiber by a substantial amount, about six ounces for every tablespoon of bran. There is little evidence to indicate that an increased consumption of fiber might be harmful. Researchers have agreed that the side effects of bran are for the most part minimal and temporary, while the benefits are numerous.

The start-up of a bran-rich diet may produce a slightly bloated feeling, increased intestinal gases, loose bowel movements for the first few days, a feeling of distention, colic, and/or possibly bad breath. Most of these symptoms are reported to be temporary, and some may never appear if the bran has been added gradually within a ten-week to sixteen-week period, according to Dr. Burkitt.

Another precaution with the increased use of fiber

concerns the absorption of minerals and vitamins by the bran. Mineral balance has been one major area where there is disagreement about the effect of fiber, particularly with the minerals calcium and zinc. It was suggested in the *Journal of Nutrition* in 1976 that fiber causes increased fecal losses of these minerals such that negative balance results, leading to detrimental physiological consequences. However, more recent studies reported in 1981 in *Advances in Lipid Research* have shown that the body has the ability to adapt to the change in diet and should have no long-term mineral imbalance. The effect of fiber on calcium balance, for example, had been found to depend on the type of fiber used; calcium was actually found to be increased in the body with the use of wheat bran in the diet. Further evidence by J. H. Cummings in the *British Medical Bulletin* in 1981 indicates that few changes in mineral balance occurred when moderate amounts of bran are added to a mixed diet of bran and natural fiber.

Many of the concerns over fiber and mineral balance are directed to particular groups of people such as the elderly, whose mineral imbalance may be due to factors other than increased bran. One of these factors, according to a National Health and Nutrition Survey in 1971–72, is use of laxatives and enemas, which tend to wash the vitamins out of the intestinal tract. The survey suggested that elderly people should be advised to avoid the use of oil-based laxatives since they tend to carry away vitamin A, and other fat-soluble vitamins, and thiamine. Bran has been identified as being preferable to the use of medications or habitual reliance on laxatives. Habitual use of laxatives has resulted in a bowel that is unable to function without stimulation; fiber has been found to produce the same effect as laxatives without crippling the system.

There is a different precaution about the purchasing of bran-fiber products or "high-fiber" products of which the public should be aware. Processed foods that label themselves as being high in fiber most often contain large amounts of fat, salt, sugar, and refined grain products as well. This includes many foods such as breads, cereals, crackers, pastries, muffins, cookies, and, especially, granola, which is higher in both fat and calorie content than most regular cereals. Therefore, cooking with processed "high-fiber" bran cereals, for instance, can double the amount of fat, sugar, and salt content of a food while adding a minimal amount of fiber to it.

The majority of fiber investigators have concluded that there is nothing to be lost by following the guidelines to increase dietary fiber, both bran and natural. Ten countries, including the United States, have made recommendations at national levels for changes in diet that should improve health. They have without exception advocated an increased consumption of fiber.

WHO NEEDS BRAN FIBER IN THEIR DIET?

While good nutrition does not in itself guarantee good health, certainly the latter cannot be achieved without the former. Good nutrition has been found to be necessary for both physical and mental health at all stages of life. Since the 1960s, the concept of health has changed from being treatment-oriented to being prevention-focused as well. Proper nutrition has been found to be a valuable aid in the prevention and/or treatment of many health disorders in young people, and, especially, in older patients. In the *Journal of Human Nutrition*, A. M. Stephan goes on to state that the best-known avoidance of health problems has consisted of trying to prevent the underlying disease, and one effective way to do this has been to normalize the operation of the digestive system by restoring essential fiber to the diet.

Retirement, which is a major life event, has presented its challenges to the older adult's nutritional status. The aim of a preventive approach to health through good nutrition is currently being seen as an attempt to keep older people as healthy as possible. For example, a study done at the Jackson Veterans Administration Medical Center found a definite vulnerability to dietary carcinogens that may increase the occurrence of cancer in the elderly. This group concluded that dietary prevention of cancer through the use of increased fiber in the diet may be effective in advanced age. Louise Davies, in the article "Healthy Retirement" in *Nursing Mirror*, suggested that men and women would benefit from good nutritional training and advice before they retire, which would in turn encourage healthier life-styles upon retirement. According to Maria Salerno, there are now twenty-three million persons who are sixty-five or older in the United States whose food habits have already been formed and whose health situations will be a result of these formed habits. It is in this group of people that major health problems most often surface.

WHY CHILDREN NEED BRAN FIBER

It is not just the elderly who need sound nutritional training. Recent research has found that both children and adults need diet direction as well. The problem of poor nutritional habits resulting in obesity has been found to affect twenty-five percent to forty percent of adults over thirty years of age and an increasing amount of young children according to Louise Davies. Not only does bran help lower the risk of appendicitis, as demonstrated by the University of Washington study in 1985, it has been used successfully to treat recurrent abdominal pain in children. When fiber was added to the child's diet, there was a significant decrease in pain attacks, or stomachaches, to the extent that there were fifty percent fewer attacks in subjects given added fiber.

Recent studies on fiber and nutrition have indicated that the increased use of fiber in the diet is becoming an accepted fact in disease prevention and health maintenance for both the young and the old. In a study conducted in the Netherlands concerning the cholesterol levels of seven- to eight-year-old boys from sixteen different countries, it was found that low-fat/high-fiber diets effectively lowered the cholesterol levels of the subjects involved. The test, reported in *Preventive Medicine*, further concluded that "western" diets, which were found to be high in fat and low in fiber, were responsible for elevating cholesterol concentrations in children and in young adults. Of even greater concern is the fact that the disease diverticulosis apparently takes about forty years to damage the intestinal wall, so the ideal time to have begun to avoid the irreversible damage is during childhood.

Another study done by the Department of Medicine at the Louisiana State University Medical Center examined the dietary intake of carbohydrate and fiber in 148 children randomly selected from a biracial community. Comparative studies done over a three-year period of the children, ten to thirteen years of age, showed that fiber intake was greater in the black children than in the white children, but none of the children's intake of fiber was compatible with prudent dietary recommendations. In the study "Fiber Intake and Childhood Appendicitis" published in the *American Journal of Public Health*, J. Brender et al.

reported that children with a fiber-rich diet had a fifty percent lower risk of appendicitis than those who had a low-fiber diet. The conclusions of most studies point out the need for bringing practical nutritional practices to as wide a cross-section of age as possible. In particular, the studies done by Louise Davies point to a need for practical fiber-rich everyday food for the entire family.

WHY CHANGE TO A HIGH-FIBER DIET?

Research suggests that the longer we delay changing a low-fiber diet to a high-fiber diet, the greater the chances that one or several health problems will occur. Although good nutrition has been recognized as essential to maintenance of health and the prevention of disease, the quality and quantity of the foods one selects is rarely based solely on meeting the basic need for good health through nutrition. Education, religion, culture, and socioeconomic status have all been shown to have an extremely strong influence on dietary patterns. This has been found to be especially true with the older adult.

According to C. Murphy in an article concerning the nutrition of the older adult in *Nutrition News*, individuals fifty-five to sixty-five years of age and older have established patterns of meeting their nutritional needs and they pass these patterns on to the next generation. More often than not, these patterns are the result of poor nutritional knowledge and the effects of misleading and oftentimes deceptive advertising of food and nutrition products. This can be attested to by the fact that forty percent of employees in domestic worksites are overweight and seventy percent practice poor nutrition. Murphy went on to express a need for a way to change the dietary patterns of the older adult, and he also expressed the need for early education in good nutritional habits for younger adults.

Other researchers have cited a need for change in the dietary habits of older patients. M. J. Hill has pointed out in the article "Dietary Fat and Human Cancer" in the *Proceedings of the Nutrition Society* that the need to assess dietary intake retrospectively arises primarily because the effects of diet on tumor growth are said to occur long before the growth becomes clinically manifest. The interval between the effect of diet and a health problem can be as short as one year to as many as ten to twenty years. Furthermore, Hill has suggested that the dietary habits of people change from year to year, some to a greater extent than others, and it could be this change that sound nutritional education could affect.

Dr. Burkitt in 1984 strongly suggested that change to a fiber-rich diet has become necessary for every western culture. As he stated the situation: "To those of us who have concentrated on the treatment of gastrointestinal disease to the almost total exclusion of prevention, the words of the American poet Ogden Nash might be applicable: 'We are making great progress, but we are headed in the wrong direction!' "

❧ 6 ❧

The Oat and Wheat Bran Health Plan

ADD YOUR BRAN TO A FAVORITE DISH

Surveys show that most families rely on a handful of recipes for the majority of their meals. Most of these recipes are family favorite dishes. This diet can be made more healthful by simply adding bran to it. The secret is knowing how and when to use bran in the preparing of these dishes so that the family will get the necessary fiber and still want to eat the dish.

A major consideration pointed to in suggesting a family diet that would increase the use of bran was that the diet must be a palatable and enjoyable one. For as A. M. Stephan put it in the article "Should We Eat More Fiber?" in the *Journal of Human Nutrition*, there is little point in advising people to eat large amounts of bran if they find it dry and tasteless and are likely to give it up. Stephan went on to advise that especially children, who need added bran the most, will be the first to not eat it if they don't like it, regardless of whether or not it is good for them.

THE WHEN, HOW, AND WHY IN USING BRAN

TAKE ALL THE THINGS THAT YOU LIKE TO EAT AND MAKE THEM BRAN-NEW!

FIRST: *WHEN to add bran to your diet:*

1. Brown bran along with chicken, meat, turkey, or fish when frying, barbecuing, roasting, or baking.
2. Always use bran as part of the flour ingredient for cakes, breads, cookies, and muffins.
3. Add to commercial mixes for cakes, muffins, meat mixes, and meat coatings to make low-fiber food into high-fiber food.
4. Use bran for breading meat and fish.
5. Sprinkle bran on hamburger patties, roasts, spareribs, ground beef and pork, chops, and steaks while cooking.
6. Use bran instead of bread crumbs in any recipe, as on top of casseroles, in dressings, meat loaf, and so forth.
7. Use bran as a thickening tool in soups, gravies, dressings, casseroles, sauces, and stews.
8. Use bran in everything you can as you cook.

SECOND: *HOW to add bran to your diet*:

The amount of bran to use and the method for using it will vary with each type of recipe. *The Oat and Wheat Bran Health Plan* recipe section includes examples of many types of foods so you can learn how to use bran in any type of recipe. Once you are acquainted with these methods and amounts, you will be able to improvise for yourself, using your own favorite recipes.

Remember, though, to keep the bran in a readily visible container so you will be reminded to use it every day as you prepare meals. For example, keep the bran in a glass container in the refrigerator, on the kitchen counter, beside the stove, or wherever you can easily spot it. Of course, use bran in packaged foods as well as home-prepared foods.

Here are some *amounts* to keep in mind as you add bran fiber to food:

There are about five grams per teaspoon.

Two to three tablespoons is thirty to forty grams.

There are about three teaspoons to one tablespoon of bran.

There are about twenty-four teaspoons (8 tablespoons) to one-half cup of bran. (So, for example, in the Breakfast Cookie recipes, there is approximately one teaspoon of bran per cookie.)

When using packaged mixes, add from ¼ to ½ cup of bran plus the same amount of added liquid. For example, for meat "helper" mixes, and ¼ cup of bran plus ¼ cup liquid; for cake, muffin, and pancake mixes, add ¼ to ½ cup bran plus liquid, depending on your preferences. (See Desserts, Cake Mix Sample Recipe.)

THIRD: *WHY to add bran to your diet*:
1. To help prevent serious illness: The National Cancer Institute will spend $1.2 billion looking for a cure for cancer, but the best prevention is changing your diet.
2. To control weight and provide energy: This is a diet that you can live with because it's your choice of food prepared with *The Oat and Wheat Bran Health Plan* method.
3. Because it's easy to do: If you know that you can easily add bran to your diet right now, why should you wait until next month?
4. Because you have to eat, so make it good for you: Eat as though your life depends on it, because it does.
5. Because your whole family will benefit: Adults need bran now for treatment and children need bran now for prevention.

While using the recipes in this book, maintain one constant thought: *Make one food in one meal contain bran at least once every day!*

TEN STEPS TO A BRAN-NEW HEALTH PLAN

1. Use bran to lower cholesterol and prevent and treat serious disease.
2. Start with one teaspoon of bran a day.
3. Use bran in one food in one meal at least once every day.
4. Drink more water.
5. Continue to eat fruits and vegetables as well.
6. Take time to adjust your system to bran.
7. Add bran to both home-cooked food and packaged food.
8. Use bran to control weight and provide energy.
9. Buy bran in bulk form to save money.
10. Take all of the things that you like to eat and make them "bran-new"!

Begin your Bran Health Plan today. Start with the Breakfast Cookies as a way to introduce bran to your family and yourself. In the Breakfast Cookie recipes, there is approximately one teaspoon of bran per cookie, so it is easy to keep track of how much bran each person is getting. Breakfast Cookies are irresistible to both children and adults and a practical way to get everyone to experience the fact that *The Oat and Wheat Bran Health Plan* can be a delicious plan.

All the recipes tell you the amount of bran per serving, so that as you begin adding bran to your daily meals, you can keep a record of how much your family is getting in the course of a day.

The proportion of wheat bran and oat bran to add to your Bran Health Plan is up to you. All the recipes in *The Oat and Wheat Bran Health Plan* have been tested for both kinds of fiber. So you can decide how much of each bran you wish to use in your health plan. If you want to concentrate on cholesterol levels with your Bran Health Plan, then use oat bran; if you are concerned about intestinal problems, colon cancer, diverticulitis, gallstones, and the like, then use wheat bran. As medical information suggests, it is best to use a combination of both oat bran and wheat bran in order to insure for yourself and your family the greatest amount of benefit. You are then getting the benefit of oat bran and its protection from cholesterol as well as the benefit of wheat bran and its protection for the intestinal areas with increased transit speed.

WHERE TO GET UNPROCESSED BRAN

Bran is available as fiber in bulk form in supermarkets and health food stores. The oat bran and wheat bran can be purchased by the bagful found in bins in the self-service areas. This is the most economical way to buy bran, especially when you intend to cook with it on an ongoing basis. Oat bran is usually about three times the price of wheat bran.

Bran can also be purchased in prepackaged boxes in most food stores. This is a more expensive way to buy bran than in bulk form. To get the benefits of bran, it is necessary to use a low-processed or unprocessed fiber. Be careful not to think that by using a bran cereal or a bran-fiber mix that you will be getting the same effect for your health plan as with unprocessed bran, because packaged bran cereals often contain extra fat, sugar, and salt.

HOW TO GET STARTED ON THE OAT AND WHEAT BRAN HEALTH PLAN

A bran-fiber-full health diet would include thirty to forty grams of fiber daily, that is, two to three tablespoons. It is best to begin to use bran fiber slowly.

For Adults:
1. Start with a teaspoon per day (about five grams).
2. Slowly increase the amount to two or three table-spoons per day (thirty to forty grams).
3. Implement this program over a ten- to sixteen-week period.

For Children between five and twelve years of age:
1. Start with one-half teaspoon per day.
2. Slowly increase the amount to about one table-spoon per day.
3. Implement this plan over a ten- to sixteen-week period.

For Children between three and five years of age:
1. Needed daily amount is about one-half to one teaspoon.
2. Most young children will get the needed amount from a portion of the prepared family food.

Start gradually and allow your system time to adjust. You will find that as soon as you begin to use bran you will be satisfied with less food, have energy for a longer period of time, and will be hungry less often, not to mention more regularity and ease with your bowel functions.

GETTING STARTED ON THE OAT AND WHEAT BRAN HEALTH PLAN

The Oat and Wheat Bran Health Plan presents an easy-application method that will show you how to use bran in the preparing of food so that your entire family can get the necessary fiber per day, almost without their knowing it. The recipes in *The Oat and Wheat Bran Health Plan* recipe section are easy to read and easy to prepare. Most of the recipes can be prepared in twenty to thirty minutes. The consumer research director at General Mills reports that if a meal takes more than thirty minutes to prepare, people don't want to deal with it, and yet people want to eat real food.

Most families have a few favorite recipes and meals that they repeat over and over. This is a collection of everyday recipes made fiber rich and healthful. Families have to eat, so make it healthful. Find your favorite family recipe in this book and you will be surprised that you can have the same favorite dishes, only now they're protectors of your health as well.

QUESTION: How long should I use this Bran Health Plan?
ANSWER: As long as you want to feel good!

For further information about what foods will add dietary fiber, refer to the chart Foods Rich in Dietary Fiber, a listing of fiber-food sources (Appendix A). This chart lists the amount of fiber in grams per hundred grams in foods that contain fiber. For example, as listed, wheat bran flour contains 44.0 grams of fiber per hundred grams of flour (or about three ounces), while white flour contains only 3.15 grams of fiber per hundred grams. It is interesting to note the amount of fiber that is present in bran flour in relation to any other food source.

See also the listing of fiber sources that are suggested by the Nursing Division at St. Luke's Regional Medical Center, Boise, Idaho (Appendix B). This chart, Diet Information and Suggestions for a High-Fiber Diet, lists the amount of grams per food in individual measurements such as cups, ounces, and so on. This chart also gives information on water intake, exercise, and fiber side effects.

7

The Oat and Wheat Bran Health Plan Recipes

Breakfast Cookies

Oatmeal Breakfast Cookies

❦

Makes 4 dozen cookies
Bran per cookie: 1 teaspoon

These cookies are a dream come true for kids and other people who tend to skip breakfast. Even if the people at your house don't like oatmeal, they'll love these cookies. Make them very large for a quick and easy oatmeal breakfast.

> ¾ cup soft margarine (or light olive oil)
> 1 cup brown sugar
> 2 eggs, beaten (or 3 egg whites)
> 3 tablespoons molasses
> ½ cup low-fat (1%) milk
> 1 cup whole wheat flour
> 1 cup **bran**
> ¾ teaspoon baking soda
> 1 teaspoon salt
> 2 cups quick-cooking oats
> 1 to 2 cups raisins

1. Preheat oven to 375 degrees. Have ready a greased cookie sheet.
2. Blend margarine or oil, sugar, eggs, molasses, and milk.
3. Add flour, bran, baking soda, and salt, and mix well.
4. Blend in oats and raisins.
5. Drop large tablespoonfuls onto prepared cookie sheet.
6. Bake at 375 degrees for 10 to 12 minutes.

❧ BREAKFAST COOKIES

Breakfast cookies are for:

People who want to eat healthier—fast!
People who work.
People who are busy.
People who have no time for breakfast.
People who have children who don't like breakfast.
People who live alone and don't make breakfast.
People who want a breakfast that is ready to go.
People who need a high energy start in the morning.

Cookies for breakfast may seem too good to be true—but they're good for you and always ready to eat. These super cookies have the same important nutrients any good breakfast has. When you serve them with milk, you have the same nutrients you get in breakfast cereal, but with far fewer additives. Each cookie in the following recipes contains about 1 teaspoon of bran per cookie, so you can easily get a good start on your daily fiber requirement or fill it completely.

As my teenager says: "Cookies make a great breakfast; put a bunch of them in your book bag and eat them in math class!"

Peanut Butter Breakfast Cookies

❦

Makes 3 dozen cookies
Bran per cookie: 1 teaspoon

These cookies have almost zero cholesterol. To make the cookies more crispy, leave out the milk.

½ cup soft margarine (or light olive oil)
1 cup smooth or chunky peanut butter
1 cup brown sugar
1 egg, beaten (or 2 egg whites)
1 cup whole wheat flour
¼ cup low-fat (1%) milk
1 cup **bran**
½ teaspoon baking powder
¾ teaspoon baking soda
¼ teaspoon salt

1. Preheat oven to 350 degrees. Have ready a greased cookie sheet.
2. Blend margarine or oil, peanut butter, sugar, and egg.
3. Add the rest of the ingredients and mix well.
4. Roll into 2-inch balls, the size of Ping-Pong balls.
5. Place on prepared cookie sheet and press flat with the tines of a fork.
6. Bake at 350 degrees for 8 to 10 minutes.

Double Chocolate Chip Breakfast Cookies

❧
Makes 3 dozen cookies
Bran per cookie: 1 teaspoon

These nicely chewy cookies are so good they'll disappear almost in front of your eyes. In fact, you may want to double the recipe, so I've given the proportions below.

> ½ cup soft margarine (or light olive oil)
> 1 cup brown sugar
> 1 egg, beaten (or 2 egg whites)
> 1 teaspoon vanilla extract
> 1½ cups whole wheat flour
> ½ cup **bran**
> ¼ cup low-fat (1%) milk
> ½ teaspoon baking soda
> ½ teaspoon salt
> ¼ cup unsweetened cocoa
> 1 cup chocolate chips

1. Preheat oven to 350 degrees. Have ready a greased cookie sheet.
2. Cream together margarine or oil, sugar, egg, and vanilla.
3. Blend in the rest of the ingredients except chocolate chips.
4. Add the chocolate pieces and mix well.
5. Drop large teaspoonfuls about 2 inches apart onto prepared cookie sheet.
6. Bake at 350 degrees for 10 to 12 minutes.

DOUBLE RECIPE

1 cup soft margarine (or light olive oil)
2 cups brown sugar
2 eggs, beaten (or 3 egg whites)
2 teaspoons vanilla extract
3 cups whole wheat flour
1 cup **bran**
½ cup low-fat (1%) milk
1 teaspoon baking soda
1 teaspoon salt
½ cup unsweetened cocoa
2 cups chocolate chips

Follow directions above. For extra-large breakfast cookies, bake 4 to 5 minutes longer.

❧ USING SUGAR

Brown sugar is usually called for in these recipes, and it doesn't matter whether it's light brown sugar or dark—your choice; dark brown sugar has a little more molasses in it and will give a slightly stronger flavor. If you need to cut down on sugar, try using half as much as the recipe specifies—the recipes are designed to work with those amounts. But also be honest with yourself; if there isn't an urgent medical reason to cut down on sugar, don't. Remember that if you don't like the taste of the food, chances are you won't make the recipe again. And if this bran plan doesn't become a life-style for you, it won't do you much good. These recipes are family-tested, and they've passed muster with the toughest critics a cook has—your kids will like them too, guaranteed.

Raisin and Bran Breakfast Cookies

❧

Makes 4 dozen cookies
Bran per cookie: 1½ teaspoons

If this recipe sounds familiar, it's because these are the Raisin and Bran Muffins (see page 213), our family's favorite, in cookie form for a quick-start and convenient breakfast.

> 2 tablespoons soft margarine (or light olive oil)
> ½ cup brown sugar
> 1½ cups whole wheat flour
> 1½ cups **bran**
> 1 cup low-fat (1%) milk
> 1 cup molasses
> 1 teaspoon baking soda
> 1½ teaspoons cinnamon
> ½ teaspoon salt
> 1 egg, beaten (or 2 egg whites)
> 1 teaspoon vanilla extract
> 1 cup raisins (2 cups if you love raisins)

1. Preheat oven to 375 degrees. Have ready a greased cookie sheet.
2. Combine margarine or oil and sugar.
3. Add remaining ingredients and mix well.
4. Drop from tablespoon onto prepared cookie sheet.
5. Bake at 375 degrees for 8 to 10 minutes.

Banana Breakfast Cookies

❦

Makes 4 dozen cookies
Bran per cookie: 1 teaspoon

These large cookies are like little banana cakes. They're not only full of bran, they also have a healthy amount of potassium too.

> ¾ cup soft margarine (or light olive oil)
> 1 cup brown sugar
> 2 eggs, beaten (or 3 egg whites)
> 1 cup mashed ripe bananas (about 2 to 4, depending on size)
> ½ cup low-fat (1%) milk mixed with 1 teaspoon baking powder
> 1 teaspoon vanilla extract
> 2½ cups whole wheat flour
> 1 cup **bran**
> ½ cup molasses
> 1 teaspoon cinnamon (optional)
> 1½ teaspoons baking soda
> ½ teaspoon salt
> 1 to 2 cups raisins (optional)

1. Preheat oven to 375 degrees. Have ready a greased cookie sheet.
2. Blend margarine or oil, sugar, eggs, and bananas.
3. Add remaining ingredients and mix well.
4. Drop large tablespoonfuls onto prepared cookie sheet.
5. Bake at 375 degrees for 10 minutes.

Applesauce Breakfast Cookies

Makes 4 dozen cookies
Bran per cookie: 1 teaspoon

Make your own variation, using any canned fruit pureed in a blender—crushed pineapple, pears, and peaches all work very well.

¾ cup soft margarine (or light olive oil)
1 cup brown sugar
2 eggs, beaten (or 3 egg whites)
¾ cup applesauce
1 cup **bran**
2 cups whole wheat flour
½ cup molasses
½ teaspoon baking soda
½ teaspoon salt
1 teaspoon cinnamon
¼ teaspoon ground cloves
1 to 2 cups raisins

1. Preheat oven to 375 degrees. Have ready a greased cookie sheet.
2. Blend margarine or oil, sugar, eggs, and applesauce.
3. Add the rest of the ingredients and mix well.
4. Drop large tablespoonfuls onto prepared cookie sheet.
5. Bake at 375 degrees for 10 minutes.

Brown Sugar Breakfast Cookies

❧   Makes 3 dozen cookies
                         Bran per cookie: ½ teaspoon

These cookies can be made festive by adding 1 cup of
chopped colored gumdrops for the holidays. You can
use red and green gumdrops for Christmas, orange
gumdrops for Halloween, or multicolor for Easter.

> ⅔ cup soft margarine (or light olive oil)
> 1 cup brown sugar
> 1 egg, beaten (or 2 egg whites)
> 1 teaspoon vanilla extract
> ½ teaspoon baking soda
> ½ teaspoon salt
> 1½ cups whole wheat flour
> ½ cup **bran**
> 2 tablespoons low-fat (1%) milk

1. Preheat oven to 350 degrees. Have ready an un-
   greased cookie sheet.
2. Cream together margarine, sugar, and egg.
3. Add remaining ingredients; mix well.
4. Roll into 2-inch balls and flatten on cookie sheet.
5. Bake at 350 degrees for 10 minutes.

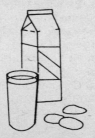

❧ STIRRING BRAN INTO OTHER FOODS

Because it takes a while for bran to absorb moisture—and if it doesn't, your recipe won't work—it's important to stir it in slowly, allowing an extra minute or so for the moisture to enter the bran. For the same reason, you'll always need a little extra liquid in the recipe—often it's easily provided by not draining thawed frozen vegetables, for instance, or including the canning juices of the food you're adding.

Pumpkin Breakfast Cookies

❦

Makes 4 dozen cookies
Bran per cookie: ½ teaspoon

These are a nice treat for cold fall mornings. Besides, this is a good way to use up the leftover pumpkin from pie-making.

    2 cups whole wheat flour
    ½ cup **bran**
    ¼ teaspoon nutmeg
    ½ to 1 teaspoon cinnamon
    2¼ teaspoons baking powder
    ¼ teaspoon ground cloves
    ¾ cup soft margarine (or light olive oil)
    1 cup brown sugar
    1 egg, beaten (or 2 egg whites)
    1⅓ cups mashed pumpkin
    ¼ cup low-fat (1%) milk
    1 to 2 cups raisins

1. Preheat oven to 350 degrees. Have ready a greased cookie sheet.
2. Combine first six ingredients and mix well.
3. Blend in remaining ingredients.
4. Drop from a teaspoon (tablespoon for large cookies) onto prepared cookie sheet.
5. Bake at 350 degrees for 15 to 20 minutes.

❧ WHY CHILDREN NEED BRAN

Bran has traditionally been the province of the older population, who use it simply to facilitate their digestion. But studies show that it's equally important for children—a study at the University of Washington, for instance, indicated that attacks of appendicitis were cut in half in children who ate bran regularly. We also know that in childhood the groundwork is laid for atherosclerosis, diverticulitis, and other medical conditions, not to mention bad eating habits. We've raised three very healthy children on bran and we recommend that as soon as a child is old enough to eat a cookie, it should be a bran cookie.

Fudge-Nut Refrigerator Breakfast Cookies

Makes 4 dozen cookies
Bran per cookie: ½ teaspoon

Here is an easy, do-ahead recipe that's great to have on hand. The dough will keep in the refrigerator for at least 1 month. Slice and bake as needed. Children love to help roll and make these fudge cookies.

¾ cup soft margarine (or light olive oil)
1 cup brown sugar
1 egg, beaten (or 2 egg whites)
1 teaspoon vanilla extract
½ cup unsweetened cocoa
½ teaspoon salt
½ teaspoon baking soda
½ cup **bran**
2 cups whole wheat flour
1 cup hot water
½ cup finely chopped walnuts

1. In a large bowl, mix together the margarine or oil, sugar, egg, vanilla, and cocoa.
2. Add the salt, baking soda, bran, flour, and hot water, and blend well.
3. Stir in the nuts and divide the dough in half in the mixing bowl.
4. Place each half of the dough on a generous piece of plastic wrap, roll into a 2-inch diameter roll, wrap, and chill for 2 hours or longer.
5. When ready to bake, preheat oven to 350 degrees. Have ready a greased cookie sheet.

6. Allow dough to warm for 10 to 20 minutes. Cut in ¼-inch slices, flatten into wafers with a glass, and place on prepared cookie sheet.
7. Bake at 350 degrees for 8 to 10 minutes. Don't overbake.

❧ THE EASIEST COOKIES

Almost all the cookie recipes in this book are extremely easy to make, but they'll be even simpler if you can avoid a messy cleanup. Cover the cookie sheet with a sheet of aluminum foil and drop the cookies right on it. There is no need to grease the cookie sheet (or the foil).

Chewy Gingersnap Breakfast Cookies

❦

Makes 4 dozen cookies
Bran per cookie: ½ teaspoon

People seem to love the chewiness of bran cookies. These are spicy, chewy, and satisfying. Roll mixture into large balls (3 to 4 inches) for large breakfast cookies.

> ¾ cup soft margarine (or light olive oil)
> 1 cup brown sugar
> 1 egg, beaten (or 2 egg whites)
> ¼ cup molasses
> 1½ cups whole wheat flour
> ½ cup **bran**
> 2 teaspoons baking soda
> ½ teaspoon salt
> 1 teaspoon ginger
> ½ teaspoon ground cloves
> 3 tablespoons low-fat (1%) milk
> 1 to 2 cups raisins (optional)

1. Blend margarine or oil, sugar, egg, and molasses.
2. Add remaining ingredients.
3. Cover dough and set in refrigerator for 1 to 2 hours.
4. Preheat oven to 350 degrees. Have ready a greased cookie sheet.
5. Roll dough into 2-inch balls and place about two inches apart on prepared cookie sheet.
6. Bake for 8 to 10 minutes at 350 degrees. (Don't overbake.)

Breakfast Drinks

Yogurt Shake

🐛

Makes 2 servings
Bran per serving: 1 tablespoon

You may want to double or triple this recipe, since the shake keeps well in the refrigerator for several days. You may use ¼ to ½ cup any fresh fruit in place of the banana.

> 1 cup plain low-fat yogurt
> 1 ripe banana, peeled and cut in chunks
> 2 tablespoons **bran**
> ¼ to ½ cup low-fat (1%) milk (as desired for
>   thickness)

1. Place ingredients in a blender.
2. Blend well and serve.

Fruit Cooler

❦

Makes 2 servings
Bran per serving: 1 tablespoon

This bubbly shake gives a bright start to the morning.
You can substitute ¼ to ½ cup of fresh strawberries
or raspberries for the orange.

> 2 tablespoons non-fat dry milk
> 2 tablespoons **bran**
> 1 egg
> 1 orange, peeled and sectioned
> 1 banana, peeled and cut in chunks
> ¼ cup sparkling mineral water
> 1 tablespoon honey (optional)
> 2 ice cubes

1. Add all ingredients to blender container.
2. Blend at top speed for 1 minute, until well mixed
   and frothy.

Mocha Whirl

Makes 2 servings
Bran per serving: 1 tablespoon

This is a tasty coffee drink that will get you off to a good start in the morning.

> 1 cup (8 ounces) coffee-flavored low-fat yogurt
> 1 cup low-fat (1%) milk
> 2 tablespoons **bran**
> 1 teaspoon sugar-free cocoa mix

1. Combine yogurt, milk, bran, and cocoa mix in a blender container.
2. Cover, whirl until mixed, and serve immediately.

Other Breakfast Ideas

Sausage Muffins

🐛

Makes 12
Bran per muffin: 1 teaspoon

These are great hearty breakfast muffins that reheat
well.

>1 pound Italian sausage, crumbled
>¾ cup **bran**
>1½ cups whole wheat flour
>1 tablespoon baking powder
>1 teaspoon baking soda
>1 teaspoon salt
>1 teaspoon pepper
>⅓ cup light olive oil
>⅔ cup buttermilk

1. Preheat oven to 450 degrees. Have ready a greased 12-cup muffin tin.
2. Brown sausage and ¼ cup bran together in a skillet for 15 to 20 minutes.
3. Mix remaining bran and other ingredients and blend well.
4. Drain and fold the sausage mixture into the batter.
5. Spoon into prepared muffin cups and bake at 450 degrees for 15 minutes.

Peanut Butter Muffins

❧

Makes 12 muffins
Bran per muffin: 2 teaspoons

These muffins are just like having a peanut butter sandwich for breakfast, only better.

1½ cups whole wheat flour
½ cup **bran**
2 teaspoons baking soda
1 teaspoon salt
2 cups (16 ounces) plain low-fat yogurt
½ cup peanut butter, smooth or chunky
½ cup brown sugar
1 cup raisins

1. Preheat oven to 350 degrees. Have ready a greased 12-cup muffin tin.
2. Mix flour, bran, soda, salt, and yogurt.
3. Add remaining ingredients and blend well.
4. Drop mixture into prepared muffin tin, filling the muffin cups to their tops for large muffins.
5. Bake at 350 degrees for 40 minutes. Remove from oven and allow to cool.

Cinnamon Coffee Cake

❦

Serves 6
Bran per serving: 4 teaspoons

This is one of those cakes that smells heavenly while it's baking. It's a great coffee cake, but it can also work as a dessert—just serve it warm with a dab of whipped cream.

⅓ cup soft margarine (or light olive oil)
1 cup brown sugar
2 eggs, beaten (or 3 egg whites)
1 cup whole wheat flour
½ cup **bran**
1 teaspoon baking powder
1 tablespoon cinnamon
½ cup low-fat (1%) milk

1. Preheat oven to 350 degrees.
2. Blend together the margarine or oil, sugar, and eggs.
3. Add remaining ingredients and mix well.
4. Pour into an 8×8-inch or 9×9-inch glass baking dish.
5. Bake at 350 degrees for 30 to 35 minutes. Allow to sit for 5 to 10 minutes before cutting.

Bran-New Pancakes

🍒

Makes 4 servings
Bran per serving: 4 teaspoons

You can make these pancakes any size you like. My family prefers silver-dollar-size pancakes.

> 1 egg, beaten
> 1½ cups buttermilk (or sour milk)
> 1 tablespoon light olive oil
> ⅓ cup **bran**
> 1 cup whole wheat flour
> 1 tablespoon brown sugar
> 1½ teaspoons baking powder
> ½ teaspoon baking soda
> ½ teaspoon cinnamon
> ½ teaspoon salt

1. Heat a pancake griddle or heavy skillet.
2. Mix together the egg, milk, and oil (in a blender or by hand).
3. Add remaining ingredients and blend well.
4. Ladle pancakes onto heated and greased griddle.
5. Cook until bubbles appear on the surface, then turn to brown on other side.

Eggs Florentine

🍎

Serves 4 to 6
Bran per serving: 1½ teaspoons

Eggs Florentine sounds very elegant, and in fact this dish looks like a lot of work, but actually it's very easy, and great for brunch. If you have cholesterol problems, pass it by.

> 1 (10-ounce) package frozen chopped spinach, thawed
> ½ cup **bran**
> 1 jar (8 ounces) Cheez Whiz
> 4 to 6 eggs (1 egg per half-slice serving)
> 2 to 3 English muffins split and toasted
> Grated Parmesan cheese

1. Combine spinach, bran, and Cheez Whiz in saucepan over low heat.
2. Poach eggs in simmering water for 3 to 5 minutes, until yolks begin to set.
3. Spoon spinach mixture on each English muffin half and top with a poached egg.
4. Sprinkle Parmesan cheese on top and serve immediately.

Double Bran Oatmeal Cereal

❦

Serves 2
Bran per serving: 1½ teaspoons

Interest your whole family in breakfast again with a new variation on an old-fashioned breakfast with a double-good start. Instead of raisins, try apples, bananas, or even peaches.

> 1⅓ cups water
> ¼ teaspoon salt (optional)
> ⅔ cup quick-cooking oats
> 1 tablespoon **bran**
> ⅓ cup raisins or diced fresh fruit (optional)
> 1 tablespoon brown sugar (optional)
> Milk

To microwave:
1. Stir together all ingredients except milk in a glass bowl or a 2-cup glass measuring cup.
2. Microwave on high for 2 minutes.
3. Mix well before serving with milk.

For stove-top cooking:
1. Bring water to brisk boil, add salt and stir in oats.
2. Cook 1 minute. Add remaining desired ingredients except milk and stir occasionally.
3. Remove from heat, cover, and let stand 3 to 5 minutes or until oatmeal reaches desired consistency. Serve with milk.

Appetizers

Deviled Eggs

🍒

Serves 6
Bran per serving: 1 to 1½ teaspoons

It's surprising how much people love humble deviled eggs. If you don't have cholesterol problems, eggs are nutritious, and this recipe uses a lot of bran too.

> 6 hard-cooked eggs, peeled
> ½ cup light mayonnaise or yogurt
> 2 to 3 tablespoons **bran**
> Season to taste with: salt, pepper, lemon pepper
> seasoning, garlic powder
> ½ cup minced scallions, radishes, or cucumbers
> (optional)
> Chopped parsley or paprika

1. Cut cooked eggs in half; remove and mash yolks.
2. Mix with remaining ingredients except parsley or paprika and refill egg-white halves with mixture.
3. Sprinkle with chopped parsley or paprika and serve.

Cocktail Meatballs

🍸
Serves 6
Bran per serving: 4 teaspoons

These tasty little meatballs can be made days in advance and frozen in a plastic bag. Thaw them before adding to the cocktail sauce.

>   1 pound lean ground beef (or ground turkey)
>   ½ cup **bran** or more
>   ½ cup tomato juice
>   1 teaspoon salt
>   ¼ teaspoon pepper
>   1 garlic clove, minced (or ½ teaspoon garlic
>   powder)
>   1 teaspoon Worcestershire sauce

COCKTAIL SAUCE:

>   1 (12-ounce) bottle chili sauce
>   1 (10-ounce) jar grape jelly

1. Mix together everything but the chili sauce and jelly and shape into ½-inch (bite-size) meatballs.
2. Place as many meatballs on a cookie sheet as it will hold. Sprinkle some extra bran on top of the meatballs for a crust.
3. Place the meatballs under the broiler until done, about 10 to 15 minutes.
4. Heat chili sauce and jelly in heatproof serving dish, stirring constantly until jelly is melted.
5. Add meatballs to sauce and stir until thoroughly coated.
6. Simmer uncovered for 20 minutes.
7. Serve in sauce with toothpicks.

Cocktail Chicken Wings

Serves 12
Bran per serving: 2 teaspoons

These little chicken wings are a good example of how bran can work to make a dish taste even better. In this case, bran makes the chicken much crispier. The recipe makes 48 little wing pieces, and although it should serve 12 people, 6 people could make short work of them too.

> 24 chicken wings
> ½ cup sherry
> ¼ cup light soy sauce
> ½ teaspoon ground ginger
> 4 garlic cloves, minced (or 2 teaspoons garlic powder)
> ½ cup **bran**
> ¼ cup grated Parmesan cheese
> 1 teaspoon lemon pepper seasoning
> 1 teaspoon garlic powder

1. Disjoint chicken wings and discard tips so that you have two pieces per wing.
2. Combine the sherry, soy sauce, ginger, and garlic. Mix well and marinate the chicken pieces for at least 1 to 2 hours.
3. Preheat oven to 350 degrees. Have ready a greased baking sheet.
4. Combine the bran, Parmesan cheese, lemon pepper seasoning, and garlic powder in a plate.
5. Remove chicken pieces from marinade, coat each piece on all sides with bran mixture, and place on prepared baking sheet.
6. Bake at 350 degrees for 20 to 30 minutes or until crisp.

Mustard Chicken Strips

🌣

Serves 4
Bran per serving: 2 tablespoons

This savory recipe can also be made with chicken parts, but they need to cook another 5 to 10 minutes.

> 2 tablespoons mustard
> 2 tablespoons honey
> 1 tablespoon fresh lemon juice
> ¼ cup apple juice (or cider)
> ¼ cup white wine (or vermouth)
> 2 garlic cloves, minced (or 1 teaspoon garlic powder)
> 2 pounds chicken strips
> ½ cup **bran**
> No-stick cooking spray for spraying dish
> Sesame seeds

1. Preheat oven to 375 degrees.
2. Mix the mustard, honey, lemon juice, apple juice, wine, and garlic together.
3. Add chicken strips and marinate at least 1 hour.
4. Put the bran on a plate and coat each chicken strip with bran.
5. Place coated chicken in a 9 × 12-inch oblong glass baking dish sprayed with cooking spray.
6. Spray coated chicken with cooking spray and sprinkle generously with sesame seeds.
7. Bake at 375 degrees for 30 to 40 minutes, or barbecue on a grill until tender.

Dips

Spinach Dip

❦

Serves 6
Bran per serving: 2 teaspoons

Dips are a painless way to get your daily bran requirements. This lovely green dip is particularly good with raw vegetables.

> 1 (10-ounce) package frozen chopped spinach, defrosted and well drained
> ¼ cup chopped scallions
> ¼ cup **bran**
> 1 teaspoon lemon pepper seasoning
> 2 garlic cloves, minced (or 1 teaspoon garlic powder) (optional)
> ½ cup light mayonnaise
> ½ cup light sour cream (or low-fat yogurt)
> Salt and pepper, to taste

1. Mix ingredients together and season to taste.
2. Serve with crackers, raw vegetables, or cocktail breads.

Hot Broccoli Dip

❧

Serves 6
Bran per serving: 4 teaspoons

This recipe requires a chafing dish or fondue pot—
it's great for buffet entertaining.

1 tablespoon soft margarine
3 celery stalks, diced
1 onion, chopped
1 (4-ounce) can sliced mushrooms (or 1 pound
    sliced fresh mushrooms)
½ cup **bran**
1 (10-ounce) package frozen chopped broccoli
1 (8-ounce) roll garlic cheese (any kind)
1 (10¾-ounce) can condensed cream of
    mushroom soup

1. In a skillet, melt the margarine and sauté the
   celery, onion, and mushrooms. Sprinkle on bran
   and sauté until soft and clear.
2. Add broccoli and cheese to mixture. (Broccoli will
   cook while the cheese melts.)
3. Add mushroom soup and heat through.
4. Place in chafing dish and keep warm while serving.
5. Serve with large chips, bread cubes, or bread
   sticks.

Guacamole Dip

🍓

Serves 4
Bran per serving: 1 tablespoon

Festive and delicious too, this dip easily disguises the bran that's in it.

> 1 large ripe avocado (or 2 small ripe avocados),
>   mashed
> 1 medium ripe tomato, diced fine
> 3 scallions, diced
> 1 tablespoon fresh lemon juice
> ¼ cup **bran**
> ¼ cup light mayonnaise (or plain low-fat yogurt)

1. Combine all ingredients and mix together well.
2. Serve with crackers or chips.

Black-Eyed Pea Dip

❦

Serves 10
Bran per serving: 1½ teaspoons

On New Year's Day in the South, black-eyed peas are essential eating to insure good luck in the year to come—and to insure everyone's good health, there's plenty of bran here too.

> 1 pound dried black-eyed peas
> 2 smoked ham hocks
> 2 onions, diced
> 8 celery stalks, chopped
> 2 red or green peppers, diced
> 1 cup **bran**
> 2 garlic cloves, minced (or 1 teaspoon garlic powder)
> 1 teaspoon oregano
> 1 bay leaf
> 1 teaspoon black pepper
> 1 tablespoon brown sugar (or maple syrup)

1. Rinse black-eyed peas in hot water.
2. Brown the ham hocks in a large cooking pan.
3. Add onions, celery, and peppers.
4. Add the black-eyed peas and enough water to cover.
5. Simmer covered for about 2 hours.
6. Add remaining ingredients.
7. Stir occasionally and continue to simmer about 1 more hour, until thickened slightly.
8. Remove the ham bones when the meat has cooked off, dice the meat, and return it to the peas.

9. Remove from heat and allow to cool. The peas will thicken as they cool.
10. Spoon into smaller portions and serve hot or cold with corn chips, pita chips, or crackers.

❧ COUNTING OUT YOUR BRAN

Sometimes it gets confusing to sort out the teaspoons, tablespoons, and cups of bran you're using to make sure you get the right amount. Here are the formulas:

¼ cup = 12 teaspoons or 4 tablespoons
½ cup = 24 teaspoons or 8 tablespoons
1 cup = 48 teaspoons or 16 tablespoons
⅓ cup = 16 teaspoons or 5 heaped tablespoons

Everyone over 5 years old in your family should be getting 2 to 3 tablespoons of bran a day. Under 5, it's a teaspoon a day.

The Short-Cut Version of Black-Eyed Pea Dip

❦

Serves 6
Bran per serving: 4 teaspoons

If the previous recipe for black-eyed peas sounded good but time-consuming, try this one. This dip makes a great New Year's Day gift. Place a small jar of dip tied with a ribbon in a basket along with a small bag of chips, and give abundant good luck. You'll also be helping your friends to healthful eating.

> 1 (11-ounce) package of frozen black-eyed peas
> 1 to 2 cups chopped canned ham
> 1 (10-ounce) can chicken broth
> ½ cup **bran**
> 2 onions, diced
> 8 to 10 celery stalks, chopped
> 2 red or green peppers, diced
> 2 garlic cloves, minced (or 1 teaspoon garlic powder)
> 1 teaspoon oregano
> 1 teaspoon pepper
> 1 tablespoon brown sugar

1. Combine all ingredients in a large saucepan and simmer 30 to 40 minutes, until peas are tender.
2. Stir occasionally and continue to simmer until slightly thickened.
3. Allow to cool and thicken further. Serve hot or cold.

Spicy Bean Dip

❦

Serves 4
Bran per serving: 1 tablespoon

This zippy dip can be made ahead of time and re-heated or brought to room temperature. Use the small measurement of bran if you are new to using bran fiber in your diet, and then increase the amount as you wish.

1 can (16 ounces) refried beans
¼ to ½ cup **bran**
¼ to ½ cup salsa
½ cup tomato juice
2 garlic cloves, minced (or 1 teaspoon garlic powder)
2 to 3 celery stalks, diced

1. Combine all ingredients and mix well.
2. Serve hot or at room temperature with pita triangles or corn chips.

Mild Bean Dip

❧

Serves 4
Bran per serving: 2 tablespoons

If you don't like spicy food, this bean dip will taste just right. Children particularly love this mild version.

> 1 can (16 ounces) refried beans
> ½ cup **bran**
> ¼ cup tomato juice or tomato sauce
> ¼ cup catsup (or tomato paste)
> 2 garlic cloves, minced (or 1 teaspoon garlic powder)
> 2 to 3 celery stalks, diced

1. Combine all ingredients and mix well.
2. Serve hot or cold with pita triangles or corn chips.

Skinny Mexican Chip Dip

❦

Serves 6
Bran per serving: 4 tablespoons

A lot of Mexican dips are quite fattening, but not this one. To keep it skinny, hold back on the chips and serve it with slices of green pepper.

> ½ pound lean ground beef (or ground turkey)
> ½ cup finely chopped onion
> ½ cup **bran**
> 2 garlic cloves, minced (or 1 teaspoon garlic powder)
> 1 (8-ounce) can tomato sauce plus 2 to 3 cans water (as desired for thickness)
> 1 cup low-fat cottage cheese
> ½ teaspoon oregano
> Grated Parmesan cheese

1. In a skillet, brown meat, onion, and bran. Add garlic.
2. Add remaining ingredients except Parmesan cheese and mix together with meat mixture until heated through.
3. Place in serving dish and sprinkle Parmesan cheese on top.
4. Serve with pita chips, green pepper slices, or corn chips.

Soups

Clam Chowder

❦

Serves 4
Bran per serving: 1 tablespoon

This satisfying chowder should be served with crackers or a crusty bread and salad.

>2 slices bacon, diced
>¼ cup onion, chopped
>6 large unpeeled potatoes, scrubbed and diced
>⅓ cup **bran**
>2 (6½-ounce) cans minced clams with their juice
>1 quart package dry milk
>1 quart water
>¼ teaspoon salt
>¼ teaspoon pepper

1. Sauté bacon over medium heat in a 3- or 4-quart cooking pot.
2. Add onions and potatoes and sprinkle on bran while cooking for 10 minutes.
3. Add the clams and juice, dry milk, and water. Mix together well to dissolve powdered milk.
4. Add salt and pepper and allow to simmer 10 to 15 minutes, until potatoes are cooked. Do not boil.

Turkey and Corn Chowder

❦

Serves 4
Bran per serving: 2 tablespoons

Corn chowder has long been an American favorite. This recipe takes it one more step. Serve with a tossed salad and it's a complete meal. Each serving has your daily bran requirement.

> ¼ pound ground turkey
> 1 medium onion, chopped
> 2 medium unpeeled potatoes, scrubbed and chopped
> ½ cup **bran**
> 1 teaspoon salt
> ½ teaspoon pepper
> 1 quart low-fat (1%) milk (or 4 cups water plus 1 quart package dry milk)
> 2 (16-ounce) cans whole-kernel corn with its juice

1. In a large heavy saucepan over medium heat, brown ground turkey, onion, and potatoes together, sprinkling on the bran while browning.
2. Add seasonings and milk; simmer 15 minutes.
3. Add corn and liquid and cook over medium heat for an additional 20 to 30 minutes.

Potato and Onion Soup

🐛
Serves 4
Bran per serving: 1 tablespoon

This soup can be served in bread bowls: hollow out small round loaves of bread, bake on a cookie sheet at 350 degrees for 10 minutes, and fill with soup.

> 3 to 4 large unpeeled potatoes, scrubbed and diced
> 2 bunches scallions, diced, or 2 onions, chopped
> 1 cup diced celery
> 2 tablespoons soft margarine (or light olive oil)
> ⅓ cup **bran**
> 2 garlic cloves, minced (or 1 teaspoon garlic powder)
> ½ to 1 teaspoon pepper
> 1 quart water
> 1-quart envelope non-fat dry milk

1. Sauté the diced potatoes, scallions, and celery in the margarine or oil in a heavy 4-quart cooking pot over medium heat.
2. Sprinkle bran on vegetables as they sauté, until transparent.
3. Add seasonings to vegetable mixture.
4. Add water and dry milk to vegetables and mix well.
5. Simmer gently for 15 minutes.

Stews

Chili

❦

Serves 4
Bran per serving: 4 tablespoons

Your family will never suspect that they're getting their much-needed bran in this all-time favorite dish.

> ½ pound lean ground beef
> 1 cup **bran**
> 2 onions, chopped
> 2 green peppers, chopped
> 3 to 4 cups ripe tomatoes (or 1 [6-ounce] can tomato paste plus 3 cans water or 2 [8-ounce] cans tomato sauce plus 2 cans water or 1 can [1 pound 13 ounces] whole tomatoes)
> 1 bay leaf (optional)
> 1 to 2 teaspoons chili powder, to taste
> 2 teaspoons salt
> 1 or 2 15-ounce cans kidney beans, undrained
> 1 tablespoon maple syrup (optional)

1. Brown the ground beef in a heavy 4-quart cooking pot, sprinkling the bran on the meat as it browns.
2. Add onions and peppers to mixture.
3. Add remaining ingredients and simmer uncovered 1 to 2 hours.
4. Add more liquid if necessary.

Chuck Wagon Stew

❦

Serves 6
Bran per serving: 1½ tablespoons to 3 tablespoons

1 pound beef stew meat cut in 1-inch chunks
½ to 1 cup **bran**, to taste
1 to 2 tablespoons olive oil, if necessary
1 medium onion, chopped
2 cloves garlic, minced (or 1 teaspoon garlic
    powder)
1 teaspoon lemon pepper seasoning
1 teaspoon Worcestershire sauce
2 cups carrots, scrubbed and chopped
2 cups potatoes, scrubbed and chopped
1 (1-pound) can tomatoes

1. Slowly brown meat and bran together in a large 4-
   to 6-quart cooking pot, using oil if necessary.*
2. Add chopped onion and seasonings. Continue to
   brown slowly for 10 minutes.
3. Cover meat mixture with water. Add carrots,
   potatoes, and tomatoes.
4. Add 3 to 4 cups water as desired for thickness and
   mix stew together well.
5. Cover and simmer for 1 to 2 hours.

*If you brown the meat with a lid on the cooking pot you may not
need to use the olive oil.

❧ STORING BRAN

In the refrigerator, bran will keep almost indefinitely.
But it's important to keep it in a glass jar on your
kitchen counter, so you'll remember to use it as often
as possible.

Winter Squash Stew

❧

Serves 6
Bran per serving: 1½ to 3 tablespoons

This is a thick stew much like a spaghetti sauce; it can be served in a soup bowl over spaghetti noodles—even children love squash made this way.

> 1 pound ground turkey meat
> ½ to 1 cup **bran**, to taste
> 1 to 2 tablespoons olive oil, if necessary
> 1 cup chopped celery
> 1 large onion, chopped
> 1 to 2 (4-ounce) cans mild green chilies, diced
> 2 to 4 cloves garlic, minced (or 1 to 2 teaspoons garlic powder)
> 1 teaspoon Mrs. Dash lemon and herb seasoning
> 1 teaspoon lemon pepper seasoning
> 4 cups winter squash (or pumpkin), peeled and cubed
> 1 (6-ounce) can tomato paste

1. In a 4- to 6-quart cooking pot, slowly brown together the ground meat and bran, using oil if necessary.*
2. Add the chopped celery, onion, chilies, and seasonings, and continue to brown for 10 minutes.
3. Add the cubed squash and tomato paste. Add 4 to 6 cups water.
4. Cover and allow to simmer 2 to 3 hours, or until squash is tender. Stir occasionally as it simmers.

*If you brown the meat with a cover on the cooking pot, you may not need to use the oil.

Mexican Stew

❦

Serves 4
Bran per serving: 2 tablespoons

Serve this stew with corn bread and you have a complete Southwestern meal.

> 1 pound stewing beef, cut in cubes
> ½ cup **bran**
> 1 to 2 tablespoons olive oil, if necessary
> ¼ cup light soy sauce
> 1 teaspoon oregano
> 3 garlic cloves, minced (or 1½ teaspoons garlic powder)
> ½ teaspoon ground cumin
> 2 cups chopped carrots
> 1 cup chopped green pepper
> 2 medium ripe tomatoes, chopped
> 2 medium onions, chopped
> 1 (8-ounce) can whole-kernel corn plus juice

1. In a 4- to 6-quart cooking pot, slowly brown the meat and the bran together, using oil if necessary.*
2. Add soy sauce, seasonings, and 2 to 3 cups water.
3. Add all vegetables and mix together well.
4. Cover pot and allow to simmer for 30 minutes to 1 hour. Stir occasionally.

*If you brown the meat with a cover on the cooking pot, you may not need to use the oil.

Turkey Noodle Stew

❦

Serves 6
Bran per serving: 4 teaspoons

This homey recipe is a great way to use the leftover holiday turkey, plus any leftover vegetables such as celery, onions, or carrots.

> 2 whole turkey legs (or turkey thighs or 3 to 4 cups chopped turkey meat)
> ½ cup **bran**
> 2 quarts water (or vegetable stock to cover turkey)
> 1 teaspoon pepper
> 1 teaspoon salt
> 1 teaspoon dried basil
> 1 teaspoon celery seeds
> 2 garlic cloves, minced (or 1 teaspoon garlic powder)
> 1 bay leaf
> 1 clove
> 2 cups diced carrots
> 2 cups diced celery
> 1 (12-ounce) package noodles

1. In a heavy, covered 4-quart cooking pot, brown the turkey meat on all sides, sprinkling on bran as it browns.
2. Cover the turkey with water or vegetable stock.
3. Add seasonings and simmer until the turkey is cooked, about 1 to 2 hours. Remove meat from bone if necessary.
4. Add vegetables to liquid and meat. Cook 15 to 20 minutes.
5. Add uncooked noodles and cook 15 to 20 minutes or until done.
6. Add more liquid (water) if desired, as noodles will absorb much of the liquid while cooking.

Barley Beef Stew

❦

Serves 6
Bran per serving: 4 teaspoons

This is a great cold weather meal; just add a salad
and you're all set.

    1 pound stew meat
    1 tablespoon light olive oil, if necessary
    ½ cup **bran**
    1¼ cups barley
    4 to 6 cups liquid (water, broth, or vegetable
        stock)
    Salt and pepper, to taste
    2 cups diced carrots (optional)

1. Brown meat in a 4-quart heavy cooking pot, using
   oil if necessary.* Add bran to the meat while it
   browns.
2. Add barley and brown mixture 3 to 5 more minutes, until well browned.
3. Add liquid and seasonings.
4. Add carrots if desired.
5. Simmer 1 to 2 hours. Barley will absorb liquid, so
   add more if desired.

*If you brown the meat with a cover on the cooking pot, you may
not need to use the oil.

MAIN DISHES

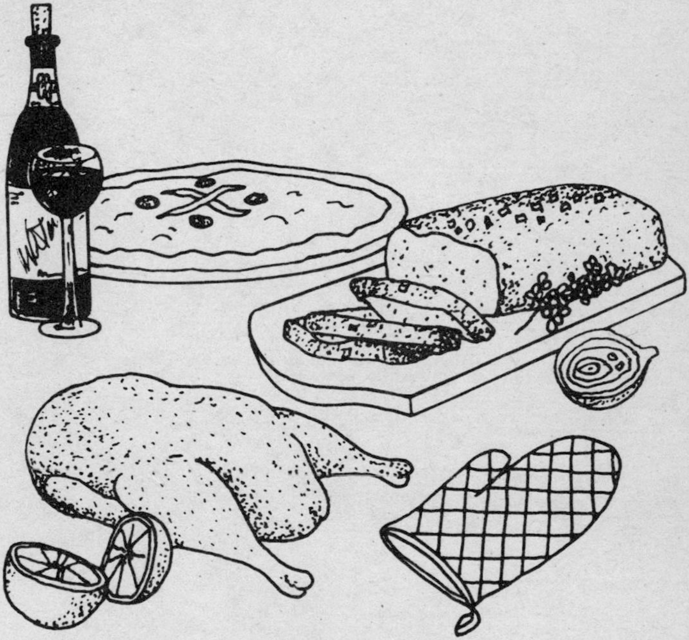

Beef, Pork, and Veal

Spanish Rice Bake

❦

Serves 4
Bran per serving: 2 tablespoons

This meal in one dish can be made ahead and baked at your convenience. Bake for 5 to 10 minutes longer if casserole is cold when beginning to bake.

> 1 pound lean ground beef
> ½ cup **bran**
> 1 to 2 tablespoons olive oil, if necessary
> 1 medium onion, diced
> ½ to 1 cup diced green pepper
> 2 cups canned tomatoes
> 1 tablespoon Worcestershire sauce
> 2 garlic cloves, minced (or 1 teaspoon garlic powder)
> 1 teaspoon lemon pepper seasoning
> ½ teaspoon oregano (optional)
> 2 cups cooked rice

1. Preheat oven to 350 degrees.
2. In an ovenproof serving dish or casserole, brown the ground beef and bran together over medium heat, using oil if necessary.*
3. Add the diced onion and green pepper while browning.
4. Add the tomatoes and seasonings and mix well.
5. Add cooked rice and blend together.
6. Bake at 350 degrees for 20 to 25 minutes.

*If you brown the meat with a cover on the cooking pot, you may not need to use the oil.

Beef Stroganoff

❦

Serves 4
Bran per serving: 2 tablespoons

In place of the sour cream you might expect to find in this recipe, I use small-curd cottage cheese, which works very well and turns a very rich dish into a healthful one. The cottage cheese melts into the sauce—but be sure to use small-curd cottage cheese; this trick won't work with the large-curd kind.

1 pound lean beef strips, cut for stir-frying
1 to 2 tablespoons olive oil
½ cup **bran**
2 cups beef broth (low sodium if available)
½ cup tomato sauce
1 teaspoon dry mustard
¼ teaspoon oregano
¼ teaspoon pepper
2 tablespoons dry wine (optional)
1 cup small-curd cottage cheese
½ pound mushrooms, washed and sliced
1 medium onion, chopped
1 (12-ounce) package noodles, cooked

1. In a heavy skillet over medium-high heat, brown beef strips in oil, sprinkling bran on all sides of the meat as it browns.
2. Add the beef broth and simmer, stirring constantly to thicken.
3. Add the tomato sauce, seasonings, wine, and cottage cheese, and mix thoroughly.
4. Add mushrooms and onion and allow to simmer 20 minutes, or until cottage cheese has melted.
5. Stir occasionally to maintain constant thickness of sauce, and serve over cooked noodles.

Chili Meatballs

🐦
Serves 4
Bran per serving: 4 tablespoons

If you want to make this recipe even easier, use canned chili—the bran is already in the meatballs.

1 pound lean ground beef (or ground turkey)
1 cup **bran**
1 cup tomato juice (or 1 [8-ounce] can tomato sauce)
1 garlic clove, minced (or ½ teaspoon garlic powder)
½ teaspoon chili powder
1 (15-ounce) can stewed tomatoes
1 (15-ounce) can kidney beans plus their juice
1 teaspoon chili powder
1 (12-ounce) package noodles, cooked

1. Mix first 5 ingredients together and shape into 1-inch meatballs.
2. Brown meatballs slowly in a skillet over medium heat.
3. Combine and heat the stewed tomatoes, kidney beans, and chili powder in a heatproof serving dish.
4. Add meatballs to heated tomato-chili sauce and serve over cooked noodles.

Spaghetti and Meat Sauce

🍂

Serves 4
Bran per serving: 2 tablespoons

Spaghetti is a favorite in almost every house. Here are two ways to make this meal even more healthful for the entire family: use ground turkey in place of beef, and, of course, use bran. There's also a meatless spaghetti recipe on page 159.

MEAT MIXTURE:

½ pound lean ground beef (or ground turkey)*
½ cup **bran**
½ cup minced onion

Sprinkle ground meat with bran and brown together in a heavy skillet over medium heat. (Sprinkle bran on all sides of ground meat while browning.) Add onion.

🍂 BROWNING MEAT AND BRAN TOGETHER

If you add the bran along with the meat and brown them together, the bran will form a delicious crust. Not only does it look exactly like the meat alone, but it almost doubles the quantity, so you can use much less meat. If you usually make spaghetti sauce with a pound of ground meat, for instance, you can use a half pound of meat along with a half cup of bran and you'll have the same volume. Bran also works as a thickening agent in the spaghetti sauce so you don't have to add flour.

SAUCE:

1 (1½-ounce) package spaghetti mix, or make
    your own, using oregano, basil, thyme,
    garlic, salt, and pepper
1 (8-ounce) can tomato paste (or 8 to 10 fresh ripe
    tomatoes)
2 cups water, or use vegetable juices drained from
    canned vegetables
1 (1-pound) carton cottage cheese
1 (4-ounce) can mushrooms with their juice
1 (12-ounce) package spaghetti, cooked and
    drained
Grated Parmesan cheese

1. Add all ingredients except cooked spaghetti and
   cheese to meat mixture and simmer to desired
   consistency.
2. Serve over cooked spaghetti.
3. Sprinkle Parmesan cheese on top of each serving.

*Add 1 to 2 tablespoons of olive oil if you're using turkey. Or, use
a nonstick skillet or cover your skillet.

Swedish Meatballs and Gravy

❦

Serves 6
Bran per serving: 2 tablespoons

This easy dinner can be cooked and served in one dish.

1 pound lean ground beef (or ground turkey)
½ pound pork sausage
1 egg (or 2 egg whites)
¾ cup **bran**
¾ cup low-fat (1%) milk
1 teaspoon salt
¼ teaspoon pepper
2 garlic cloves, minced (or 1 teaspoon garlic powder)
¼ to ½ cup diced onion

GRAVY:

⅛ cup **bran**
⅛ cup flour
2 cups water
2 teaspoons low-sodium beef bouillon

Cooked noodles or rice

1. Mix together the ground meat, sausage, egg, bran, milk, seasonings, and onion.
2. Shape into meatballs, about 2 tablespoons of meat mixture each, and brown on all sides in a heat-proof serving dish.
3. Remove meatballs from cooking dish. Mix together the gravy ingredients.

4. Stirring constantly, add bran mixture to drippings. Mix thoroughly and cook over low heat, adding extra water if needed.
5. Replace meatballs and heat through. Serve over noodles or rice.

❧ COOKING MEAT WITH BRAN:

—Sprinkle bran on chicken parts, steaks, chops, and cutlets, and brown.
—Sprinkle bran on meat or poultry when baking.
—Mix bran into ground meat and brown.
—Mix into meat loaf or meatballs, and bake.
—Use as breading for chicken, ribs, and fish.
—Sprinkle on meat as you barbecue. Some of the bran will stick to the meat and some will not; not to worry.

Baby Meatballs with Cauliflower

❦

Serves 4
Bran per serving: 2 tablespoons

This main dish cooks up quickly and is no-fail—it *always* works.

> 1 pound ground turkey (or lean ground beef)
> ½ cup **bran**
> 2 garlic cloves, minced (or 1 teaspoon garlic powder)
> 1 to 2 tablespoons olive oil, if necessary
> 1 small head cauliflower, separated into florets
> 1 green pepper, chopped in 1-inch pieces
> ¼ cup light soy sauce
> 1½ cups beef broth (or bouillon)
> ½ teaspoon brown sugar
> 1 tablespoon cornstarch
> 3 to 4 cups cooked rice
> ½ cup diced scallions (optional)

1. Combine the meat, bran, and garlic together and form ½-inch meatballs.
2. In a heavy skillet over medium heat, brown the meatballs on all sides—use oil if necessary.
3. Add the cauliflower, green pepper, and soy sauce. Stir to coat with soy sauce and simmer 5 to 10 minutes.
4. Blend together beef broth, sugar, and cornstarch; add to meat and vegetables. Cook and stir until thickened.
5. Serve over cooked rice and sprinkle scallions on each serving if desired.

Grandma Jewell's Stuffed Meatballs

❧

Serves 6
Bran per serving: 2 teaspoons

This dish can be done ahead of time to step 6. After placing meatballs in dish, cover with plastic wrap and refrigerate or freeze until ready to cook.

> 1 (6-ounce) box prepared stuffing
> ¼ cup **bran**
> 1 pound lean ground beef (or ground turkey)
> ½ cup evaporated milk
> ½ cup additional **bran**
> 1 (10¾-ounce) can condensed cream of
>   mushroom, chicken, or celery soup
> ¼ to ½ cup water

1. Preheat oven to 350 degrees.
2. Prepare stuffing according to package directions; add ¼ cup bran and mix.
3. Combine meat, milk, and the additional ½ cup bran.
4. Divide meat mixture into six meatballs.
5. Flatten meatballs, place a full tablespoon of stuffing in center, draw meat over stuffing, and seal.
6. Place meatballs in a 9 × 12-inch baking dish.
7. Combine soup and water and pour over meatballs.
8. Bake uncovered for 1 hour at 350 degrees.

Meatballs and Brown Rice

🍎

Serves 4
Bran per serving: 2 tablespoons

A savory and hearty combination, this main course is a favorite. You can also serve the meatballs over noodles.

        1 pound lean ground beef (or ground turkey)
        ½ cup low-fat (1%) milk
        1 teaspoon salt
        ¼ teaspoon pepper
        ¼ teaspoon garlic powder
        1 egg
        1 teaspoon Worcestershire sauce
        ½ cup grated Parmesan cheese
        ½ cup **bran**
        Spaghetti and Meat Sauce (page 122) or Bran-New
            Gravy (page 228)
        2 cups cooked brown rice

1. Mix first nine ingredients together and shape into 1-inch balls. Brown in skillet over medium heat, sprinkling some bran on the meatballs as they brown, to make a crust.
2. In a 1- or 2-quart saucepan or serving dish, heat Spaghetti and Meat Sauce or Bran-New Gravy. (You may also use a gravy mix.)
3. Add the meatballs and serve over cooked brown rice.

Meat and Potato Moussaka

❦

Serves 4
Bran per serving: 2 tablespoons

Moussaka can be an extremely rich dish, but this one is relatively light. It reheats very well, so make it ahead of time.

> ½ to 1 pound lean ground beef (or ground turkey)
> ½ cup **bran**
> 1 medium onion, chopped
> 2 medium potatoes, scrubbed and sliced
> 1 (8-ounce) can tomato sauce
> ½ teaspoon salt
> ½ teaspoon pepper
> 1 garlic clove, minced (or ½ teaspoon garlic powder)
> 2 eggs (or 3 egg whites)
> 1 cup plain yogurt

1. Preheat oven to 350 degrees.
2. In a large ovenproof baking dish over medium heat, slowly brown the meat, bran, and onion together.
3. Add the potatoes, tomato sauce, and seasonings. Cook for 5 minutes, stirring constantly.
4. Spread mixture evenly on the bottom of the dish.
5. In a mixing bowl, beat together lightly the eggs and yogurt. Spread over mixture.
6. Bake at 350 degrees for 1 hour, or until the topping is set.

Wontons

❧

Serves 6
Bran per serving: 2 tablespoons

If you've never made wontons before, you'll find it's not only easy but also fun. These also make a wonderful appetizer, and they keep beautifully in the freezer.

> 1 pound lean ground beef (or ground turkey or pork)
> ¾ cup **bran**
> 1 teaspoon dried ginger
> 2 tablespoons brown sugar
> 1 tablespoon light soy sauce
> 2 garlic cloves, minced (or 1 teaspoon garlic powder)
> 1 teaspoon sherry (or wine)
> 1 teaspoon sesame oil
> ½ cup chicken (or beef) broth
> 1 teaspoon salt
> ½ cup minced scallions
> ½ cup bean sprouts
> ½ cup shredded carrots (optional)
> 2 (8-ounce) packages wonton skins

1. Combine the first 10 ingredients and mix well.
2. Mix in vegetables and allow to stand 5 to 10 minutes.
3. Place a full teaspoonful on each wonton skin and fold up sides of the skin so that opposite sides touch at the top, then press all corners together.
4. *To cook crispy wontons:* Place on greased baking pan and bake in 400-degree oven for 15 to 20 minutes, depending on how crisp you like them.

5. *Steamed wontons:* Place in steamer rack lined with lettuce leaves to prevent the wontons from sticking. Place the filled rack over a pan of boiling water and steam for 15 to 20 minutes.

❧ BRAN AND YOUR ENERGY LEVEL

One of the best things about using bran on a daily basis is that you'll find you have much more energy, and it's much more sustained. Bran evens out the release of sugar into the bloodstream; as a result it lengthens the span of energy you get from your food, and it also avoids the immediate highs and lows that only encourage you to eat more sweets.

Mexican Pizza

❧

Serves 6
Bran per serving: 4 teaspoons

Although this dish has nothing to do with pizza (it got its name in California) it's a great-looking dish that can be a whole meal or a cocktail snack for a large group of people. You serve it on the dish it's made in, so choose a pretty, heatproof plate.

> 1 pound lean ground beef (or ground turkey)
> ½ cup **bran**
> 1 (16-ounce) can refried beans

OPTIONAL INGREDIENTS:

> ½ (16-ounce) bottle taco sauce
> 1 (4-ounce) can chopped chilies, drained

1. Brown ground meat and bran together in a skillet over medium heat.
2. Spread refried beans on a 12- to 14-inch ovenproof plate.
3. Sprinkle browned meat mixture over beans and add taco sauce and chilies if you're using them.
4. Microwave for 5 to 7 minutes or bake 15 to 20 minutes in the oven at 350 degrees. (The dish can be prepared in advance to this point and reheated before proceeding.)

TO SERVE:

4 ounces each shredded Monterey Jack and
Cheddar cheese
1 pint sour cream (or yogurt)
1 to 2 ripe tomatoes, chopped
1 cup chopped ripe olives
1 cup Guacamole Dip (page 97)
1 to 2 large (16-ounce) bags tortilla chips

1. Sprinkle cheeses on warmed meat mixture.
2. Pour sour cream in the middle.
3. Make a circle of chopped tomatoes and a second circle of chopped ripe olives around sour cream.
4. Pour Guacamole Dip on top of sour cream.
5. Serve with plenty of chips.

Tacos

❦

Serves 4
Bran per serving: 2 tablespoons

If you prefer soft-shelled tacos, just warm two tortillas at a time between two paper towels in the microwave oven for 30 seconds.

> ½ pound lean ground beef (or ground turkey)
> ½ cup **bran**
> 1 (1½-ounce) package taco seasoning or:
> ¼ teaspoon chili powder
> ½ teaspoon garlic powder
> ½ teaspoon oregano
> ¼ cup minced onion (or more to taste)
> ¾ cup water
> 10 taco shells

1. Brown the meat and bran together in a heavy skillet over medium heat.
2. Add seasonings.
3. Add the water and mix well. The mixture will be moist but not thin.
4. Put the meat mixture into taco shells and add desired toppings: grated cheese, sliced lettuce, chopped onion, diced tomato.

Fajitas

❦

Serves 4
Bran per serving: 1 tablespoon

1 pound beef or chicken strips, cut for stir-frying
¼ cup dry wine
4 tablespoons light soy sauce
2 garlic cloves, minced (or 1 teaspoon garlic
    powder)
1 teaspoon lemon pepper seasoning
1 tablespoon lemon juice
1 to 2 tablespoons olive oil, if necessary
¼ cup **bran**
2 green peppers, thinly sliced
1 onion, thinly sliced
1 to 2 tomatoes, cut in eighths
6 to 8 flour tortillas
Shredded cheese—Monterey Jack or Cheddar
1 (16-ounce) can refried beans
Salsa

1. Marinate meat strips in a mixture of wine, soy
   sauce, garlic, lemon pepper, and lemon juice for
   30 minutes to an hour. Drain, reserving marinade.
2. Heat a heavy skillet over medium high heat and
   brown meat, sprinkling bran on all sides. Use oil
   if necessary. Add 4 to 5 tablespoons of the marinade to the browning mixture.
3. Add green peppers, onion, and tomatoes to
   browned mixture and cook 3 to 5 minutes.
4. Warm flour tortillas between paper towels in
   microwave for 30 seconds.
5. Serve with cheese, warm refried beans, and salsa.

Mexican Meatloaf Squares

❧

Serves 6
Bran per serving: 2 tablespoons

I'm always looking for one-dish meals that can be made ahead, since I'm never quite sure when my husband the doctor will finally get home for dinner. This is a good one; the meatloaf part can be made ahead of time, adding the topping later; just cook 20 to 30 minutes at step 6.

1½ pounds lean ground beef (or ground turkey)
¾ cup **bran**
½ cup tomato juice
1 egg (or 2 egg whites)
1 teaspoon salt
1 teaspoon pepper
1 teaspoon chili powder
1 small onion, diced

TOPPING:

2 tablespoons soft margarine
1½ tablespoons whole wheat flour
1½ tablespoons **bran**
1 teaspoon salt
1 cup low-fat (1%) milk
8 slices American cheese (or ½ pound, grated)
1 (12-ounce) can whole-kernel corn, drained
1 to 2 green peppers, cut into 8 rings each

1. Preheat oven to 350 degrees.
2. Combine meat-loaf ingredients and mix well.
3. Pack in bottom of 9 × 12-inch baking dish and bake at 350 degrees for 20 minutes. Drain excess juice if any.

4. For topping: melt margarine. Blend in flour, bran, and salt. Add milk and bring to a boil for 1 minute. Add cheese, stir to melt, and add corn.
5. Pour topping over meat loaf and top with pepper rings.
6. Bake at 350 degrees for an additional 20 minutes. Cool before cutting.

❧ OVERCOMING THE MONOTONY OF A REGIME

As any dieter will tell you, aside from deprivation, the biggest problem with staying on a regime on a long-term basis is monotony. If you think you've solved your bran requirements with bran muffins or high-bran cereals, you may be surprised in a few months to discover that you just can't face another bran muffin, however much you like them. Our family passed through this phase long ago, and now we get our bran in a pleasing variety of dishes. Fifteen years later, we're still bran fans—variety is the secret of making bran work for you.

Meatloaf

🍂

Serves 4
Bran per serving: 2 to 3 tablespoons

Almost everyone loves meatloaf, and it's a dish that can absorb a lot of bran—and no one will even suspect you've added any bran at all. You can make one large meat loaf or several small ones.

> 1 to 1½ pounds lean ground beef (or ground turkey)
> ½ to ¾ cup **bran** to taste
> ⅓ cup low-fat (1%) milk
> ⅓ cup catsup (or tomato paste)
> 1 egg (or 2 egg whites)
> 1 teaspoon salt
> ½ teaspoon pepper

ADDITIONS:

> ½ cup shredded cheese
> ½ cup minced onions
> ½ cup minced celery
> 1 garlic clove, minced (or ½ teaspoon garlic powder)
> 1 tablespoon Worcestershire sauce

1. Preheat oven to 350 degrees.
2. Combine all ingredients, including additions, if desired.
3. Shape into 1 large loaf or 4 to 6 small loaves and place in a 9 × 12-inch baking dish.
4. Bake uncovered at 350 degrees for 50 to 60 minutes.
5. Cool for 5 minutes.
6. Use juices to make Bran-New Gravy (p. 228) if desired.

Tip: If you're making small meat loaves and you'd like to make this dish a meal, include potatoes. Cut unpeeled scrubbed potatoes in half and place two halves between each small meat loaf. Cook as directed.

❧ MIXING OAT AND WHEAT BRAN

The latest research indicates that you need both brans in your diet for optimum health. You can balance the mixture to suit your own medical concern: if cholesterol is the major issue, use seventy-five percent oat bran with twenty-five percent wheat bran. Just mix them together well and keep the bran container visible in your kitchen so you'll remember to use it as often as possible. If you're more concerned about colon cancer, diverticulosis, losing weight, or one of the other conditions that respond best to wheat bran, then tip the balance in the other direction.

Swiss Steak

❦

Serves 6
Bran per serving: 8 teaspoons

Swiss steak is a wonderful way to use a lot of bran. You can use the same recipe with a roast or a large family steak.

> 6 bottom round steaks (or chuck steaks)
> 1 cup **bran** seasoned with salt and pepper
> 2 cups beef (or chicken) broth
> 1 to 2 tablespoons barbecue sauce

1. Preheat oven to 350 degrees.
2. Coat steaks with seasoned bran.
3. Brown steaks in skillet slowly on both sides and place in a 9 × 12-inch baking dish.
4. Combine broth and barbecue sauce and add to browning skillet.
5. Simmer sauce for 5 to 10 minutes, stirring to get bran left in pan.
6. Pour sauce over steaks and cook at 350 degrees for about 1 to 2 hours or until tender.

Beef and Green Peppers

🍎

Serves 4
Bran per serving: 1 to 2 tablespoons

This is one of our family's favorite dishes—Chinese food made easy.

1 pound beef strips, cut for stir-frying—about 2 inches long, ¼ inch thick
¼ to ½ cup **bran**, to taste
1 tablespoon cornstarch
1 teaspoon brown sugar
2 to 3 tablespoons light soy sauce, to taste
1 tablespoon dry white wine
2 tablespoons sesame (or peanut) oil
2 garlic cloves, minced (or 1 teaspoon garlic powder)
2 to 3 green peppers, cut in strips about 1½ inches long
2 cups cooked rice

1. Combine the beef strips with bran, cornstarch, sugar, soy sauce, and wine.
2. Mix well and allow to stand at least 30 minutes.
3. Heat oil in wok or heavy skillet over high heat.
4. Stir in beef mixture, add garlic and cook, stirring constantly, about 2 minutes.
5. Add green peppers; cook 1 to 3 minutes, until crisp-tender, mixing well.
6. Serve over cooked rice.

Stuffed Green Peppers

❦

Serves 4
Bran per serving: 2 tablespoons

Stuffed peppers are an American classic—and they taste even better with crunchy bran.

½ pound lean ground beef (or ground turkey)
½ cup **bran**
1 medium onion, chopped
2 celery stalks, chopped
1 teaspoon salt
1 teaspoon Mrs. Dash seasoning
½ teaspoon lemon pepper seasoning
1 egg, beaten
4 medium green peppers

1. Preheat oven to 350 degrees.
2. Mix together all ingredients except peppers.
3. Wash peppers, cut off tops, and clean out seeds.
4. Fill peppers with stuffing and replace tops.
5. Place in a 2-quart baking dish and add a little water to the bottom of the dish so that the peppers won't stick.
6. Bake at 350 degrees for one hour. Remove peppers from baking dish and reserve pan juices for sauce (recipe below).

SAUCE FOR STUFFED GREEN PEPPERS

You can serve Stuffed Green Peppers with this sauce:

Pan juices from baking dish
¼ cup catsup
1 tablespoon cornstarch
1 (4-ounce) can sliced mushrooms, drained

1. Mix all ingredients together in baking dish. Stir and allow to thicken, about 5 minutes.
2. Spoon sauce over the top of the cooked peppers or serve in a sauceboat on the side.

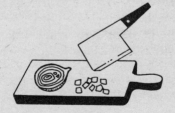

Breaded Veal Cutlets

❦

Serves 4
Bran per serving: 2 tablespoons

This main course is special enough to serve to company yet easy to prepare. You won't spend much time in the kitchen getting ready.

>   4 veal cutlets
>   ¼ cup low-fat (1%) milk
>   ½ cup **bran,** seasoned to taste (with 1 teaspoon
>   each garlic powder, basil, lemon pepper
>   seasoning, seasoned salt, or any combination
>   of seasonings)
>   No-stick cooking spray
>   ¼ cup dry white wine

1. Place each veal cutlet between two sheets of wax paper and pound to ⅛-inch thickness.
2. Dip veal in milk, then in the seasoned bran.
3. Coat heavy skillet with cooking spray and heat to medium high.
4. Place veal in pan, add wine, and cook 1 to 2 minutes per side, until golden brown.

FOR SINGLE SERVING:

>   1 veal cutlet
>   2 tablespoons low-fat (1%) milk
>   ¼ cup seasoned **bran**
>   ⅛ cup dry white wine

Prepare and cook as above.

South-of-the-Border Pork Roast

❦

Serves 6
Bran per serving: 1½ tablespoons

This easy, succulent roast will quickly become a family favorite, as it is at our house. In the final cooking, the roast acquires a delicious golden crust.

To make a complete meal, scrub medium potatoes, cut them in half, and place them around the roast as it cooks. Serve all together with sauce for gravy.

> 3- to 4-pound boneless pork loin roast
> 1 garlic clove, smashed with a knife (or ½ teaspoon garlic powder)
> ½ teaspoon chili powder
> ⅓ cup pineapple-orange or plum jelly or marmalade
> ⅓ cup barbecue sauce (or mixture of ⅓ cup catsup, 1 teaspoon vinegar, and ½ teaspoon chili powder)
> ¼ cup **bran**
> ¼ cup grated Parmesan cheese

1. Preheat oven to 325 degrees.
2. Place roast in a baking pan. Season with garlic and chili powder. Cover with foil and bake 2½ to 3 hours.
3. To make glaze, combine the jelly and barbecue sauce or catsup mixture in a small saucepan and simmer 3 to 5 minutes.
4. Remove roast from oven, baste with glaze, and sprinkle with combined bran and Parmesan cheese.
5. Return to oven uncovered and bake 30 minutes.
6. To make meat sauce, measure pan drippings and add water to make 1 cup, heat to boil, and serve with meat. (The bran will provide thickening.)

Fish and Seafood

Seafood Thermidor

❧
Serves 8
Bran per serving: 1½ tablespoons

This dish tastes very rich and is a fine addition to a buffet dinner.

> ½ pound small scallops
> ½ pound small shrimp
> ½ cup **bran**
> 8 to 10 scallions, diced
> 1 garlic clove, minced (or ½ teaspoon garlic powder)
> 1 tablespoon soft margarine
> 1 can condensed cream of shrimp or mushroom soup
> ¼ cup white wine
> ½ cup water
> ¼ cup shredded mozzarella cheese
> ¼ cup **bran**
> ¼ cup grated Parmesan cheese
> Parsley flakes
> 3 to 4 cups (or more) cooked rice

1. In ovenproof cooking dish over medium heat, sauté scallops, shrimp, ½ cup bran, scallions, and garlic in margarine.
2. Add soup, wine, and water and simmer 20 to 30 minutes.
3. Add shredded cheese and stir until melted.
4. Sprinkle ¼ cup bran on top of the seafood mixture, sprinkle the Parmesan cheese over the bran, and top with parsley flakes.
5. Broil 2 to 3 minutes, until bran crust is golden brown. Serve over rice.

Tomato-Clam Linguine

❧
Serves 4
Bran per serving: ½ tablespoon

If available, fresh clams can be substituted for the
canned variety, and for a totally different yet delicious taste, use fresh mussels.

> 2 (8-ounce) cans tomato sauce* (or 1 [28-ounce]
>   can tomatoes)
> 2 tablespoons **bran**
> 1 tablespoon cornstarch
> 6 scallions, diced
> 2 tablespoons light olive oil
> 1 garlic clove, minced (or 2 teaspoons garlic
>   powder)
> ¼ cup minced fresh parsley
> ½ teaspoon diced basil
> 2 (6½-ounce) cans minced clams
> 1 pound hot cooked linguine tossed with
>   1 tablespoon light olive oil
> Grated Parmesan cheese

1. Combine tomato sauce, bran, and cornstarch in 4-
   quart cooking pot over medium heat.
2. Add scallions, olive oil, seasonings, and clams.
3. Add cooked linguine and mix carefully.
4. Top individual servings with Parmesan cheese.

*You can also use 6 to 8 fresh ripe tomatoes.

Oven Crispy Fish Fillets

❦
Serves 4
Bran per serving: 2 to 4 tablespoons

Crispy fish is always a hit, even with people who don't usually like seafood.

> 2 pounds fish fillets, any kind, fresh or frozen
> ½ cup fresh lemon juice
> ½ to 1 cup **bran**
> ¼ cup grated Parmesan cheese
> 1 teaspoon salt and pepper
> No-stick cooking spray (or melted soft margarine)

1. Preheat oven to 350 degrees; thaw fish fillets if necessary.
2. Pour lemon juice on fish fillets in a 9 × 12-inch oblong baking dish, and set aside 5 minutes.
3. Remove fish and coat with combined bran, cheese, and salt and pepper.
4. Replace fillets in a single layer in the baking dish.
5. Spray with cooking spray or drizzle with melted margarine; add more salt and pepper to taste.
6. Bake uncovered at 350 degrees for 20 to 30 minutes.

FOR SINGLE OR SMALL SERVINGS:

> 1 to 2 fish fillets
> 1 to 2 tablespoons lemon juice
> 2 to 3 tablespoons **bran**
> 2 tablespoons grated Parmesan cheese
> 1 teaspoon salt and pepper

Prepare and cook as above.

Hot Tuna Casserole

❦

Serves 4
Bran per serving: 2 tablespoons

This crunchy version of tuna casserole is a big hit with kids. Be sure to include the canning liquid from the tuna—the bran will absorb it and it adds extra flavor.

1 (6½-ounce) can water-packed tuna, with the juices
½ cup **bran**
1 (10¾-ounce) can condensed cream of mushroom soup
1 cup (or soup can) water
1 (5-ounce) can chow mein noodles
½ cup chopped onion
½ cup chopped celery
½ cup grated Cheddar cheese

1. Preheat oven to 350 degrees.
2. Mix together all ingredients except cheese.
3. Pour into a 2-quart greased baking dish and top with grated cheese.
4. Bake at 350 degrees for 20 minutes.

Note: This dish can be made ahead of time and frozen or refrigerated until baked.

Butterfish with Spinach Stuffing

❦

Serves 4
Bran per serving: 2 tablespoons

Butterfish is extremely mild; even children like it. If rolling up fish fillets doesn't appeal to you, you can just put the stuffing mixture into the bottom of the baking dish and lay the fillets flat on top. Either way, you have a whole meal here.

STUFFING:

1 (10-ounce) package frozen chopped spinach, thawed but not drained
½ cup **bran**
½ cup chopped onion
½ cup chopped mushrooms (optional)
1 garlic clove, minced (or ½ teaspoon garlic powder)
¼ cup small-curd cottage cheese
1 teaspoon lemon pepper seasoning
½ cup grated Parmesan cheese

4 butterfish fillets (or flounder, orange roughy, etc.)
2 tablespoons white wine
½ cup grated mozzarella cheese

1. Preheat oven to 375 degrees.
2. Combine the stuffing ingredients; mix well.
3. Spoon 2 to 3 tablespoons of stuffing mixture onto each fillet and roll up.
4. Place the rest of the stuffing into a 9 × 12-inch baking dish.

5. Place the fillet rollups on top of stuffing.
6. Spoon wine over fish and sprinkle with cheese.
7. Bake covered with foil for 20 to 30 minutes at 375 degrees.

❧ CHEESES

If cholesterol is a concern, you probably won't be using any of the cheese mentioned in this book. But if you'd like to substitute a lower-fat cheese, mozzarella will work in nearly all cases. For toppings, try a light sprinkling of grated Parmesan cheese.

Hot Green Bean and Crab Bake

❧

Serves 4
Bran per serving: 1 tablespoon

This tasty dish goes together very quickly—you can use imitation crabmeat if you like.

> 2 cans green beans
> ½ pound crabmeat
> ½ cup diced onion
> ¼ cup plus 1 tablespoon **bran**
> ½ cup plain low-fat yogurt
> ½ teaspoon dry mustard
> 2 garlic cloves, minced (or 1 teaspoon garlic powder)
> Grated Parmesan cheese

1. Preheat oven to 375 degrees.
2. In a heatproof serving dish, mix together the green beans, crabmeat, and onion.
3. Add ¼ cup bran, yogurt, and seasonings and mix well.
4. Sprinkle 1 tablespoon more bran on top, then sprinkle Parmesan cheese over the casserole.
5. Bake at 375 degrees for 20 minutes.

Pasta

Noodles Romanoff

❦

Serves 4
Bran per serving: 1 to 2 tablespoons

You can use 1 cup of sour cream along with or instead of the cottage cheese if you'd like a richer dish.

> 1 recipe Bran-New gravy (page 228) (or gravy mix
>   plus ¼ to ½ cup **bran**)
> 1 cup small-curd cottage cheese
> 1 to 2 teaspoons Worcestershire sauce
> 1 garlic clove, minced (or ½ teaspoon garlic
>   powder)
> ¼ cup minced onion (optional)
> 1 (12-ounce) package cooked noodles (or pasta)

1. Combine all ingredients except noodles in a heat-proof serving dish over medium heat.
2. Mix well and cook until cottage cheese has melted.
3. Serve over cooked noodles.

Lasagna

❧
Serves 4
Bran per serving: 2 tablespoons

Easy enough for the entire family and festive enough for company, lasagna is popular with everyone.

> ½ pound lean ground beef (or ground turkey)
> ½ cup **bran**
> ½ cup minced onion
> 1 8-ounce can tomato paste plus 1 can water
> 1 cup chopped tomatoes, fresh or canned
>   (optional)
> 1 teaspoon salt (or garlic salt)
> ¾ teaspoon pepper
> ½ teaspoon oregano
> 1 8-ounce package lasagna noodles, cooked*
> ½ pound mozzarella cheese, grated
> 1 12-ounce carton low-fat cottage cheese
> Grated Parmesan cheese

1. Preheat oven to 350 degrees.
2. Brown meat and bran together in skillet over medium heat. Add onion.
3. Add remaining ingredients except noodles and cheese and simmer 20 minutes.
4. In a 9 × 12-inch baking dish, place alternate layers of cooked noodles, mozzarella cheese, cottage cheese, and sauce.
5. Bake 20 to 30 minutes at 350 degrees. Sprinkle Parmesan cheese on top and serve.

*Use whole wheat noodles for added fiber.

Lasagna in a Hurry

❦

Serves 4
Bran per serving: 2 tablespoons

This recipe is for those days when everyone craves lasagna but there isn't time to make the real thing. If you'd prefer it meatless, mix the sauce and bran together, layer with the other ingredients, and cook as directed.

> 1 pound ground beef (or ground turkey)
> 1 tablespoon olive oil (optional)
> ½ cup **bran**
> 1 medium onion, diced
> 2 (15-ounce) jars spaghetti sauce, any kind
> ¼ cup water
> 1 (12-ounce) package noodles, cooked (spinach, egg, or whole wheat lasagna noodles)
> 1 (16-ounce) carton small-curd cottage cheese
> 8 ounces grated mozzarella cheese

1. Preheat oven to 350 degrees.
2. Brown the meat, using oil if necessary, and sprinkle on the bran as the meat browns. Add the onion.
3. Add the spaghetti sauce and ¼ cup water; cook 10 to 15 minutes.
4. In a 9×12-inch baking dish, layer the noodles, meat sauce, cottage cheese, and grated mozzarella cheese. Repeat 2 to 3 times.
5. Sprinkle with Parmesan cheese and bake in a 350-degree oven for 20 to 30 minutes.

Spicy Sesame Noodles

❦

Serves 4
Bran per serving: ½ tablespoon

This delicious noodle dish has just a little bran in it—good for beginners on the Oat and Wheat Bran Health Plan. For a special touch, toast some extra sesame seeds in a skillet, being careful not to burn them, and scatter over each serving.

> 1 (10-ounce) package thawed frozen chopped broccoli, undrained
> 2 tablespoons **bran**
> 2 tablespoons light soy sauce
> 1 heaped tablespoon smooth or chunky peanut butter
> 1 tablespoon sesame oil
> 1 tablespoon sesame seeds
> 1 garlic clove, minced (or ½ teaspoon garlic powder)
> ½ cup diced scallions (optional)
> ¼ teaspoon crushed red pepper flakes (optional)
> ½ pound spaghetti (or Chinese noodles), cooked

1. Combine all ingredients except spaghetti noodles and mix together into a sauce.
2. Add sauce to cooked spaghetti or noodles and toss together.

Hot Whole-Meal Pasta

❦
Serves 4
Bran per serving: 1 tablespoon

This is a great leftovers dish—almost any vegetable will work, as will almost any meat. It's also fast—a good bet when there's no time to shop and almost no time to cook.

> ¼ cup **bran**
> ½ pound chopped meat (chicken, beef, pork, or turkey)
> 1 teaspoon Worcestershire sauce
> 1 teaspoon salt
> 1 teaspoon lemon pepper seasoning
> 1 clove garlic, minced (or ½ teaspoon garlic powder
> 1 cup *each* of any chopped vegetables, fresh or frozen: carrots, broccoli, scallions, peas, or a mixture
> 1 (12-ounce) package pasta (shells or noodles), cooked
> ½ cup ranch salad dressing

1. In a heavy 3- or 4-quart saucepan, sprinkle the bran on the meat and brown.
2. Add Worcestershire sauce and salt, lemon pepper seasoning, and garlic.
3. Place chopped vegetables on meat and allow to cook for 5 to 10 minutes, or until vegetables are tender.
4. Add cooked pasta and dressing.
5. Mix together and heat throughout.

Chilled Whole-Meal Pasta

❧

Serves 4
Bran per serving: 1 tablespoon

Here's a summer variation on the Hot Whole-Meal Pasta recipe. It's even faster because there are no vegetables to chop.

> ½ to 1 pound ground meat (chicken, beef, pork, or turkey)
> ¼ cup **bran**
> 1 teaspoon Worcestershire sauce
> 1 teaspoon salt
> 1 teaspoon lemon pepper seasoning
> 1 teaspoon minced garlic or garlic powder
> 1 (10-ounce) package frozen peas
> 1 (12-ounce) package pasta (any kind), cooked
> ½ cup ranch salad dressing (or any favorite kind)

1. In a 3- to 4-quart heavy saucepan over medium heat, brown meat and bran together.
2. Add Worcestershire sauce and seasonings; mix well.
3. Turn off heat and add frozen peas, then add pasta, cover, and allow to sit for 5 minutes.
4. Add dressing to taste to pasta mixture, toss to mix, and chill until served.

Meatless Spaghetti

❦

Serves 4
Bran per serving: 2 tablespoons

Lentils provide just as much protein as ground meat,
minus the fat.

> ¼ cup dried lentils
> ½ cup **bran**
> 1 medium onion, minced

SAUCE:

> 1 (1½-ounce) package spaghetti mix (or make
>   your own, using oregano, basil, thyme,
>   garlic, salt, and pepper)
> 1 (8-ounce) can tomato paste (or 8 to 10 fresh ripe
>   tomatoes)
> 2 cups water
> 1 (1-pound) carton small-curd cottage cheese
> 1 (4-ounce) can mushrooms with juice
> 1 (12-ounce) package spaghetti, cooked and
>   drained
> Grated Parmesan cheese

1. Simmer all ingredients together except spaghetti
   and cheese in a heavy skillet or 3-quart saucepan,
   for about 45 minutes.
2. Serve over cooked spaghetti.
3. Top each serving with Parmesan cheese.

Chicken and Turkey

Szechwan Orange Chicken

❦

Serves 4
Bran per serving: 1 tablespoon

This dish is hot and can be made even hotter by adding more red pepper flakes. It's an easy version of one of the wonderful Chinese dishes we learned to prepare when we lived in Taiwan for two years, and is a favorite of ours.

> 1 pound chicken strips, cut for stir-frying
> ¼ cup white wine
> 2 tablespoons light soy sauce
> 4 scallions, including tops, diced
> 1 teaspoon dried ginger
> 2 garlic cloves, minced (or 1 teaspoon garlic powder)
> ¼ teaspoon red pepper flakes
> ¼ cup **bran**
> 1 whole orange
> 1 tablespoon cornstarch
> 1 teaspoon brown sugar
> ½ teaspoon salt
> ¾ cup orange juice
> 1 to 2 tablespoons peanut oil
> 2 cups cooked rice

1. Combine chicken strips with wine, soy sauce, scallions, ginger, garlic, red pepper flakes, and bran.
2. Using a vegetable peeler, cut strips of peel from the orange and add to chicken mixture.

3. Mix together cornstarch, sugar, salt, and orange juice.
4. Heat peanut oil to high temperature, add chicken mixture, and cook until the chicken loses its pink color and is slightly browned. Stir constantly.
5. Add orange juice mixture, reduce heat, and cook until thickened.
6. Serve over cooked rice.

Baked Chicken and Rice

❦

Serves 4
Bran per serving: 4 teaspoons

If you're not a fan of chicken wings, you could also make this dish with chicken thighs. If you'd like to tuck in a few extra vitamins, use vegetable juices (from cooking vegetables) instead of the broth.

> 10 to 12 chicken wings
> ⅓ cup **bran**
> 3 cups low-sodium beef broth
> 1 cup brown rice, uncooked
> 1 (10¾-ounce) can condensed cream of
>   mushroom or chicken soup
> Salt and pepper, to taste

1. Preheat oven to 350 degrees.
2. Brown the chicken wings slowly in a 9 × 9-inch ovenproof baking dish, sprinkling bran on both sides of the chicken wings as they brown.
3. Remove chicken wings from dish and turn off heat.
4. Add broth and uncooked rice to baking dish. Place chicken wings on rice and spread soup over all.
5. Cover with aluminum foil and bake at 350 degrees for 1½ to 2 hours. Add more liquid during baking time if desired for softer rice. Add salt and pepper, if desired.

Stir-Fry Chicken and Chinese Noodles

❦

Serves 4
Bran per serving: 1 tablespoon

This tasty and versatile dish is very good served hot or cold; it also travels well and keeps well in the refrigerator, so can be made ahead of time.

> ½ to 1 pound chicken, diced or shredded
> 1 tablespoon sesame (or peanut) oil
> ¼ cup **bran**
> 1 garlic clove, minced (or ½ teaspoon garlic powder)
> 1 tablespoon cornstarch
> 1 teaspoon brown sugar
> ¼ cup light soy sauce
> 1 to 2 cups any chopped vegetable (fresh or frozen chopped broccoli, green pepper, green peas, snow peas, etc.)
> 1 (12-ounce) package vermicelli (or thin Chinese noodles), cooked)

1. In heavy skillet or wok, brown chicken pieces in oil, sprinkling bran on all sides of the meat as it browns. Bran will brown along with the meat and form a crust.
2. Season meat with garlic while browning.
3. Mix together cornstarch, sugar, and soy sauce; add cornstarch mixture to meat.
4. Add chopped vegetables to mixture and cook 3 to 5 minutes, until crisp-tender.
5. Add cooked noodles and cook 5 to 7 minutes, until heated through.

Almond Chicken Stir-Fry

❦

Serves 6
Bran per serving: 2 to 4 teaspoons

This dish can be prepared just as easily in a heavy
skillet or a wok. Get the whole family to help prepare
the vegetables and you'll have a delicious meal in no
time at all.

> 2 pounds chicken strips, cut for stir-frying
> 2 tablespoons sesame (or peanut) oil
> ¼ to ½ cup **bran,** to taste
> 1 diced green pepper
> 2 cups diced celery
> 4 to 5 scallions, diced
> ½ pound mushrooms, sliced
> 1 (8-ounce) can sliced water chestnuts with their
>   juice
> 1 cup blanched slivered almonds
> 1 cup beef broth (or bouillon) (low-sodium, if
>   available)
> 1 tablespoon cornstarch
> 3 tablespoons light soy sauce
> 2 cups cooked rice

1. In a heavy skillet or wok, brown chicken in oil over
   high heat and add bran to all sides of the chicken
   as it browns.
2. Add all vegetables and almonds to browning
   chicken. Reduce heat and cook 3 to 5 minutes,
   stirring constantly.
3. Mix together beef broth, cornstarch, and soy sauce
   and add to chicken and vegetable mixture.
4. Cook together 3 to 5 minutes, stirring to thicken
   evenly, adding more water if desired, and serve
   over cooked rice.

Italian Chicken with Tomatoes

❦

Serves 4
Bran per serving: 1 tablespoon

Use a cover when you brown this tasty Italian chicken
and it will be much moister.

> 1 to 2 tablespoons olive oil
> 4 single chicken breasts (or 1 pound chicken
>   strips)
> ¼ cup **bran**
> 2 garlic cloves, minced (or 1 teaspoon garlic
>   powder)
> 1 teaspoon lemon pepper seasoning
> 1 small onion, diced
> ½ pound mushrooms, washed and sliced
> 1 teaspoon dried basil
> 1 (16-ounce) can Italian-style tomatoes, including
>   juice
> 2 to 3 scallions, diced
> 2 cups cooked rice (or 1 [12-ounce] package
>   noodles, cooked)

1. Heat oil over medium heat in a heavy skillet with
   a cover.
2. Brown chicken breasts slowly, sprinkling bran on
   all sides of the chicken as it browns.
3. Add garlic, lemon pepper seasoning, onion, and
   mushrooms and cook 2 to 3 minutes.
4. Add basil, tomatoes, and juice; mix together well,
   breaking up the tomatoes as the mixture cooks.
5. Add scallions to top of mixture, cover, and simmer
   over low heat for 15 minutes. Serve over rice or
   noodles.

Chicken Burritos

❦

Serves 4
Bran per serving: 2 tablespoons

This is a make-ahead and take-along burrito dish that can be reheated in a microwave. If you'd prefer to heat the burritos in an oven, bake for 10 minutes at 350 degrees, or until warmed through.

> 1 pound diced boneless chicken
> 1 tablespoon olive oil
> ½ cup **bran**
> 5 scallions, diced
> 1 (8-ounce) can stewed tomatoes
> 2 garlic cloves minced (or 1 teaspoon garlic powder)
> 1 teaspoon chili powder
> ½ teaspoon unsweetened cocoa
> 1 (4-ounce) can diced green chilies
> 8 flour tortillas
> 1 cup grated Cheddar cheese
> 1 cup chopped lettuce
> 1 to 2 medium ripe tomatoes, diced
> Grated Parmesan cheese

1. In a heavy skillet over medium heat, brown the chicken pieces in the olive oil and sprinkle the bran on the meat as it browns—5 to 10 minutes.
2. Add the scallions, stewed tomatoes, garlic, chili powder, and cocoa; mix well.
3. Spoon 2 tablespoons of the chicken mixture and 2 teaspoons of the green chilies down the center of each tortilla. Roll tortillas and place in a 9 × 12-inch glass baking dish. Repeat procedure for all 8 tortillas.

4. Sprinkle grated Cheddar cheese evenly over the center of the tortillas, leaving 1 inch of each tortilla showing on each side.

5. Cook in microwave on medium (50 percent) power for 6 to 8 minutes, or until cheese is melted and tortillas are warmed through.

6. Spread chopped lettuce and diced tomatoes down the center of the warmed tortillas. Top with Parmesan cheese and serve.

Chicken Pot Pie

❦

Serves 8
Bran per serving: 1 tablespoon

Sprinkle extra parsley and a little grated Parmesan cheese on top of the crust to give this crowd-pleasing dish a particularly appetizing look.

2 pounds diced boneless chicken
2 to 3 tablespoons olive oil, if necessary
½ cup **bran**
1 cup chopped onion
2 cups chicken or beef broth (or bouillon)
¼ cup low-fat (1%) milk
½ teaspoon oregano
2 garlic cloves, minced (or 1 teaspoon garlic powder)
1 cup sliced mushrooms
1 cup chopped celery
1 (10-ounce) package frozen peas

1. Preheat oven to 400 degrees.
2. Brown the diced chicken in a covered skillet over medium heat; use oil if necessary. Add bran and onion while browning.
3. Add broth and milk to chicken mixture, then add seasonings.
4. Add remaining vegetables and allow to simmer 5 minutes.
5. Fold into a 9 × 12-inch baking dish.

CRUST TOPPING:

½ cup **bran**
¼ cup cornmeal
1 teaspoon brown sugar
1½ teaspoons baking powder
½ teaspoon salt
2 tablespoons soft margarine
¼ cup low-fat (1%) milk
1 egg
1 tablespoon chopped parsley

1. Combine the dry ingredients with the margarine in a small mixing bowl.
2. Add milk, egg, and parsley; mix well.
3. Spread over the top of the chicken mixture.
4. Bake at 400 degrees for 45 to 50 minutes.

Chicken Livers

🦃

Serves 4
Bran per serving: 6 tablespoons

This versatile dish works for both breakfast and dinner. Use the light gravy mix with the chicken livers for a dinner dish; the margarine sauce is best to accompany eggs for a breakfast dish. Serve the dish on toast points instead of rice if you're serving it for breakfast.

1 pound chicken livers
2 tablespoons soft margarine (or olive oil)
2 additional tablespoons soft margarine (or a light gravy mix)
¼ cup fresh lemon juice
½ cup dry white wine (or dry sherry)
1 cup water
2 cups cooked white (or brown) rice

DREDGING MIX:

1½ cups **bran**
¼ teaspoon powdered ginger
½ teaspoon seasoned salt
½ teaspoon pepper
1 teaspoon Mrs. Dash lemon and herb seasoning
½ cup grated Parmesan cheese

1. Rinse chicken livers and cut into bite-size pieces.
2. Mix dredging ingredients in a bowl or plastic bag. Add chicken livers to mixture and coat thoroughly.
3. Melt 2 tablespoons margarine or oil in a skillet or baking dish, add bran-coated livers, and cook over

medium heat for 15 minutes, until brown on all sides.

4. Add 2 more tablespoons margarine to mixture. (If using the light gravy mix, add gravy mix and ½ cup more water instead of margarine.) Add the lemon juice, wine, and water.

5. Simmer 5 minutes, until thick, stirring constantly. Add more water if necessary.

6. Serve over cooked rice or on toast points.

Chilies Rellenos Chicken

❦

Serves 4
Bran per serving: 1 tablespoon

Where we live, in the West, people adore Mexican food—we just can't seem to get enough.

> 4 whole chicken breasts, skinned, boned, and halved
> ¼ pound Monterey Jack cheese, cut in 8 equal strips
> 1 (4-ounce) can diced green chilies
> ¼ cup **bran**
> ¼ cup grated Parmesan cheese
> ½ teaspoon pepper
> ½ teaspoon salt
> ½ teaspoon chili powder (optional)
> No-stick cooking spray or ¼ cup melted soft margarine

1. Preheat oven to 425 degrees.
2. Pound chicken breasts flat to ¼-inch thickness.
3. Place a strip of cheese and 2 teaspoons of diced green chilies on each breast half and roll up.
4. Combine bran, Parmesan cheese, and seasonings in a plate.
5. Spray chicken rolls with cooking spray or dip them in melted margarine, then in bran mixture.
6. Place in ovenproof dish or pan, spread on the rest of the green chilies, and sprinkle the rest of the bran mixture on top of the chicken rolls.
7. Bake at 425 degrees for 15 to 20 minutes.

Chicken Divan Casserole

❦

Serves 6
Bran per serving: 4 teaspoons

Chicken Divan is an excellent dish for using leftover poultry. This casserole will keep well for 2 to 3 hours after baking in a low oven.

> 1 to 2 tablespoons olive oil
> 2 cups diced cooked chicken
> 2 (10-ounce) packages frozen chopped broccoli, thawed and drained
> 2 tablespoons sherry
> 1 cup plain low-fat yogurt
> 1 (10¾-ounce) can condensed cream of chicken, mushroom, or celery soup
> 2 garlic cloves, minced (or 1 teaspoon garlic powder)
> 1 cup shredded Cheddar cheese (or mozzarella cheese)
> ½ cup **bran**
> 2 tablespoons soft margarine

1. Preheat oven to 350 degrees.
2. Heat oil in a skillet and brown chicken.
3. In a glass 9 × 13-inch casserole place the broccoli, then the chicken.
4. Mix together the sherry, yogurt, soup, and garlic, and pour over the casserole.
5. Sprinkle the cheese on top of the casserole, then sprinkle on the bran, and dot with margarine.
6. Bake at 350 degrees for 30 minutes.

Chicken Curry

❦

Serves 4
Bran per serving: ½ tablespoon

Chicken curry can be a homey dish or dressed up for company—it's especially good for buffets. For a more elegant presentation, surround the curry with small bowls of chopped peanuts, chopped scallions, shredded coconut, chutney, currants, or chopped raisins, and let your guests choose their toppings.

1 pound boneless chicken, cut in 1-inch chunks
1 to 2 tablespoons olive oil
2 tablespoons **bran**
3 tablespoons soft margarine
¼ cup minced onion
1½ teaspoons curry powder
¾ teaspoon brown sugar
⅛ teaspoon powdered ginger
2 tablespoons whole wheat flour
1 heaped tablespoon **bran**
1 cup chicken broth (or chicken bouillon)
1 cup low-fat (1%) milk
½ teaspoon lemon juice
3 to 4 cups cooked rice

1. In a heavy skillet, brown the chicken slowly in the oil and sprinkle on 2 tablespoons of bran while browning.
2. Push the chicken to the edges of the skillet, and in the middle add the margarine, then the onion and seasonings. Sauté 2 to 3 minutes.
3. Blend in the flour and the 1 heaped tablespoon bran until mixture is smooth and bubbly.
4. Stir in broth and milk, stirring constantly; bring mixture to slow boil.

5. Stir cooked chicken pieces into the mixture and add lemon juice. Lower heat and add additional water for desired consistency.
6. Serve over cooked rice.

Oven Crispy Chicken

❦

Serves 4
Bran per serving: 3 tablespoons

If you love fried chicken, here's the healthful version.
This crispy chicken is also very adaptable—it's good
hot, cold, or at room temperature, and you can make
it ahead of time or at the last minute.

¾ cup **bran**
¼ cup grated Parmesan cheese
1 teaspoon lemon pepper seasoning
½ teaspoon dried basil
2 garlic cloves, minced (or 1 teaspoon garlic powder)
1 teaspoon seasoned salt
10 to 12 chicken legs (or chicken thighs)
½ cup low-fat (1%) milk
No-stick cooking spray for spraying chicken

1. Preheat oven to 350 degrees. Have ready a greased baking pan.
2. Combine bran, Parmesan, and seasonings in a plastic bag and shake.
3. Dip chicken in milk and then shake in the bag to coat with bran mix.
4. Place chicken on prepared baking pan.
5. Spray coated chicken with cooking spray for extra crispness.
6. Bake uncovered in a 350-degree oven for 1 to 1½ hours, the longer the crispier.

FOR SINGLE OR SMALL SERVINGS:

2 to 4 chicken legs (or chicken thighs)
3 tablespoons **bran**
2 teaspoons grated Parmesan cheese
1 teaspoon garlic powder, dried basil, or lemon
      pepper seasoning, as desired
¼ cup low-fat (1%) milk

Prepare according to directions above.

Artichoke and Chicken Casserole

❦

Serves 4
Bran per serving: 2 tablespoons

You can make this dish entirely in a skillet if you'd prefer; prepare as directed and simmer 45 minutes to 1 hour on top of the stove.

> 2 pounds chicken strips, cut for stir-frying
> ½ cup **bran**
> 1 (6-ounce) jar marinated artichoke hearts,
>   including the packing oil
> ½ pound fresh mushrooms, washed and sliced
> 2 garlic cloves, minced (or 1 teaspoon minced
>   garlic)
> ½ teaspoon oregano
> ½ teaspoon pepper
> 2 cups canned or fresh ripe tomatoes, chopped
> Grated Parmesan cheese
> 2 cups cooked brown rice

1. Preheat oven to 350 degrees.
2. Coat chicken pieces with bran. In a skillet over medium heat, warm the oil drained from the marinated artichoke hearts. Brown the chicken pieces in the oil.
3. Add the artichoke hearts, the mushrooms, and the seasonings to the browning chicken pieces.
4. Add the tomatoes and mix thoroughly.
5. Place mixture in a 2-quart casserole and top with Parmesan cheese.
6. Bake at 350 degrees for 1 hour and serve over the rice.

Turkey and Potato Pie

❦

Serves 4
Bran per serving: 2 tablespoons

This recipe can be doubled, baked in a 9 × 12-inch cake pan, and served in squares.

> 1 pound ground turkey
> ½ cup **bran**
> 1 cup tomato juice
> ½ cup diced celery
> ½ cup diced onion (or scallions)
> ½ cup diced green pepper
> 1 teaspoon salt
> 1 teaspoon pepper
> 1 teaspoon Mrs. Dash lemon and herb seasoning
> 3 to 4 medium potatoes, scrubbed but not peeled

1. Preheat oven to 350 degrees.
2. Combine all ingredients except potatoes and mix well.
3. Mound into a 9-inch glass pie plate or baking dish.
4. Cut potatoes into oblong quarters and place around the edge of the mounded turkey mixture.
5. Bake uncovered at 350 degrees for 50 to 60 minutes.
6. Cool 5 minutes before serving; cut into pie wedges to serve.

Savory Turkey and Noodles

❧

Serves 4
Bran per serving: 2 tablespoons

Here we have an economical main dish pasta—and it's even better when reheated the following day, so you can make it ahead.

> 1 to 2 whole turkey legs (or turkey thighs)
> ½ cup **bran**
> 1 (12-ounce) package of noodles, your choice
> 1 teaspoon salt
> 1 teaspoon pepper
> 1 teaspoon celery salt
> 1 teaspoon basil
> 2 garlic cloves, minced (or 1 teaspoon garlic powder)
> 1 teaspoon lemon pepper seasoning

1. Brown the turkey legs or thighs on all sides in a heavy 4-quart cooking pot.
2. Sprinkle bran on all sides of the turkey as it browns.
3. Cover with water and simmer until turkey is cooked, about 1 to 2 hours.
4. Remove meat from bone.
5. Add uncooked noodles to liquid and meat.
6. Season to taste with the remaining ingredients and simmer 20 to 30 minutes.
7. Noodles will cook and absorb most of liquid. Add more liquid if desired.

Dr. Tom's Wild Rice Dressing

❧

Serves 8
Bran per serving: 2 tablespoons

This is a previously secret special recipe, a family tradition at our house.

½ cup soft margarine
4 medium onions, chopped
1 bunch celery, chopped (save 2 cups)
3 green peppers, chopped
½ pound mushrooms, chopped
2 tablespoons garlic powder
2 teaspoons sage
1 tablespoon Lawry's Seasoned Salt
2 (8-ounce) packages dried Chinese mushrooms,
    soaked in water until soft
1 (12-ounce) package wild rice, cooked
1 (6¼-ounce) package Uncle Ben's Long Grain
    and Wild Rice, cooked
2 cups brown rice, cooked
1 cup **bran**

1. In a large skillet, melt margarine and sauté onions, celery, green pepper, and mushrooms. Add seasonings.
2. Soak Chinese mushrooms in water to cover until soft. Chop mushrooms small and add to sautéing vegetable mixture.
3. Combine all rices with vegetable mixture and add reserved 2 cups chopped celery.
4. Mix together well, remove from heat, and allow to stand at least 2 to 3 hours or overnight in the refrigerator.
5. Fill turkey cavities with dressing, and roast.

Baked Beans

❧

Serves 6
Bran per serving: 4 teaspoons

Everyone loves baked beans—and this dish has enough protein to be a main dish on its own. You can make it ahead of time, so it's a great dish for a potluck dinner.

> 1 (15-ounce) can red beans, drained
> 1 (15-ounce) can Great Northern beans, drained
> 1 (15-ounce) can kidney beans, drained
> 1 (15-ounce) can pork and beans
> ½ cup **bran**
> ¼ cup molasses
> ¼ cup catsup (or tomato sauce)
> ½ teaspoon dry mustard
> ½ to 1 cup chopped scallions
> ½ teaspoon baking soda

1. Preheat oven to 350 degrees.
2. Mix all ingredients together and pour in a 9 × 12-inch baking dish.
3. Bake at 350 degrees for 1 hour.
4. Allow to cool at least 20 minutes before serving.

Broccoli Casserole

❦

Serves 4
Bran per serving: 4 teaspoons

This dish bakes like a soufflé, and also can be made
with the same quantity of chopped frozen spinach.

> 2 (10-ounce) packages chopped frozen broccoli,
>   thawed and drained
> 1 egg, beaten
> 1 (10¾-ounce) can condensed cream of chicken,
>   celery, or mushroom soup
> ⅓ cup **bran**
> Grated Parmesan cheese

1. Preheat oven to 350 degrees.
2. Mix together the broccoli, egg, condensed soup,
   and bran.
3. Place mixture in a 2-quart casserole dish and top
   with grated Parmesan cheese.
4. Bake at 350 degrees for 20 to 30 minutes.

Fresh Broccoli Casserole

🍒

Serves 4
Bran per serving: 4 teaspoons

1. Steam whole head of broccoli until bright green in color.
2. Slice broccoli in 2-inch lengths and place in casserole dish.
3. Combine 1 can of creamed soup (see p. 186) with ⅓ cup bran.
4. Cover cut broccoli with soup-bran mixture and top with Parmesan cheese.
5. Bake at 350 degrees for 15 to 20 minutes, until bubbly.

Escalloped Cabbage

❧

Serves 4
Bran per serving: 1 to 2 tablespoons

This unusual recipe comes from a very old plantation cookbook—and oddly enough, it tastes like scalloped *oysters*, not cabbage.

> 1 small head green cabbage, shredded
> ¼ to ½ cup **bran**
> Salt and pepper, to taste
> Low-fat (1%) milk
> ¼ to ½ cup grated Parmesan cheese
> Soft margarine

1. Preheat oven to 350 degrees.
2. Grease a 2-quart ovenproof casserole and fill ⅔ full with shredded cabbage.
3. Add bran and season to taste with salt and pepper.
4. Cover seasoned cabbage with low-fat milk and mix all together.
5. Sprinkle Parmesan cheese on top and dot generously with margarine. Season top with salt and pepper.
6. Bake at 350 degrees for 20 to 30 minutes, or until the milk is absorbed and the top has formed a light crust.

Eggplant Parmesan

❦

Serves 4
Bran per serving: 2 tablespoons

Eggplant Parmesan is always a favorite dish; no one will even notice the extra bran tucked into the recipe.

½ cup **bran**
½ cup grated Parmesan cheese
2 garlic cloves, minced (or 1 teaspoon garlic powder)
1 medium (1½-pounds) eggplant peeled and cut into ½-inch slices
½ cup margarine, melted
1 cup pizza sauce (or spaghetti sauce)
1 cup shredded mozzarella cheese
1 tablespoon chopped fresh (or dried) parsley

1. Preheat oven to 400 degrees. Have ready a greased 9 × 12-inch baking pan.
2. Mix together bran, Parmesan cheese, and garlic.
3. Dip eggplant into margarine, coat with bran mixture, and place in prepared baking pan.
4. Spread slices generously with pizza sauce and sprinkle mozzarella cheese and parsley on top.
5. Bake at 400 degrees for 15 minutes, or until eggplant is tender.

Stuffed Mushrooms

❦
Serves 4
Bran per serving: ½ tablespoon

Stuffed mushrooms can be served immediately, of course, but they will also keep well in a warming oven.

> 12 large mushrooms
> 1 tablespoon soft margarine
> 2 tablespoons minced scallion
> 2 tablespoons minced celery
> 2 tablespoons **bran**
> ¼ cup grated Parmesan cheese
> Salt and pepper, to taste

1. Preheat oven to 375 degrees.
2. Wipe mushrooms well; remove stems and dice them.
3. In a skillet, melt the margarine and sauté mushroom stems, scallion, celery, and bran for 3 to 5 minutes. Add half the Parmesan cheese and season to taste.
4. Place mushroom caps in baking dish and fill caps with sautéed mixture. Sprinkle filled caps with remaining Parmesan cheese.
5. Bake at 375 degrees for 12 to 15 minutes.

Stuffed Potato Shells

❦

Serves 4
Bran per serving: 1 to 2 tablespoons

This hearty dish is a meal in itself—just add a salad.

4 large baked potatoes
To bake potatoes, scrub them well and prick them
several times with a fork. Bake at 350 degrees
for an hour, or until tender; or place on a
paper towel and microwave 15 minutes and
allow to stand for 3 minutes.
¼ to ½ cup **bran,** to taste
2 tablespoons low-fat (1%) milk
2 tablespoons soft margarine
½ teaspoon salt
1 teaspoon seasoned salt
2 to 3 chopped scallions
½ to 1 cup shredded Cheddar or mozzarella
cheese

1. Preheat oven to 350 degrees.
2. Cut each potato in half and scoop out center of
each half.
3. Mash potatoes and add all ingredients except
cheese.
4. Fill shells and place on baking sheet or in a 9 × 12-
inch baking dish.
5. Sprinkle shells with shredded cheese.
6. Bake at 350 degrees for 20 to 25 minutes.

Easy Spaghetti Squash

🍴

Serves 4
Bran per serving: 4 teaspoons

This dish can be a meal in itself, or can accompany a main dish as a vegetable. It has to be the simplest spaghetti squash recipe in existence, but it does take a while to cook.

1 medium (3- to 4-pound) spaghetti squash
1 cup small-curd cottage cheese
⅓ cup **bran**
½ teaspoon salt and/or garlic powder
¼ teaspoon pepper
4 to 5 scallions, diced
1 medium green pepper, diced
½ cup diced celery
½ cup diced fresh ripe tomatoes (optional)
Grated Parmesan cheese
Soft margarine

1. Place whole squash in a large cooking pot, covered, and boil gently for 30 minutes to 1 hour, until a fork can easily pierce the squash.
2. Preheat oven to 350 degrees.
3. Remove squash from water, cut in half, and scoop out the seeds and tough stringy fibers.
4. Place the cut halves in a 9 × 12-inch baking dish.
5. Mix cottage cheese, bran, and desired seasonings together and place in the center of both squash halves.
6. Mix the other vegetables together and divide in half. Add vegetables to each squash half.
7. Sprinkle liberally with Parmesan cheese and dot with margarine.

8. Bake at 350 degrees for 20 to 30 minutes, or until cottage cheese has melted and squash is heated through.
9. Remove from oven, cut halves in half again, and serve.

‌&‌ BRAN TOPPINGS

You can use bran as a topping on almost anything you'd use bread crumbs on; it will brown and form a crust. Mix a little soft margarine or Parmesan cheese or a combination of the two into the bran. If the crust doesn't brown in the oven, run it briefly under the broiler.

Hash Brown Potato Casserole

❦

Serves 6
Bran per serving: 4 teaspoons

This is a good potluck dinner dish that travels easily and reheats well.

> 2-pound package frozen hash brown potatoes
> ¼ cup melted soft margarine
> 1 cup **bran**
> 2 garlic cloves, minced (or 1 teaspoon garlic powder)
> ½ teaspoon lemon pepper seasoning
> ½ cup diced onion
> 1 (10½-ounce) can condensed golden mushroom soup
> 1 (16-ounce) carton small-curd cottage cheese
> 2 additional tablespoons melted soft margarine
> Parsley flakes

1. Preheat oven to 350 degrees.
2. In a large mixing bowl, combine hash browns, ¼ cup melted margarine, ½ cup bran, garlic, lemon pepper seasoning, onion, soup, and cottage cheese.
3. Spread mixture in a 9 × 12-inch lightly greased baking dish.
4. Combine the 2 additional tablespoons melted margarine and ½ cup bran. Spread on top of the hash brown mixture. Sprinkle top with parsley flakes.
5. Bake at 350 degrees for 1½ hours.

Scalloped Potatoes

❦

Serves 4
Bran per serving: 1 tablespoon

These scalloped potatoes are creamy, with a crunchy bran-and-cheese topping.

>4 large unpeeled potatoes, washed and thinly
>   sliced (3 to 4 cups)
>1 cup small-curd cottage cheese
>¼ cup **bran**
>Salt, pepper, and garlic powder to taste
>¼ cup low-fat (1%) milk
>½ cup grated Cheddar cheese

1. Preheat oven to 350 degrees.
2. Place potatoes in layers in a 2-quart baking dish, alternating with 2 to 3 tablespoons cottage cheese.
3. Sprinkle each layer with bran (1 to 2 teaspoons per layer) and desired seasonings.
4. Add remaining cottage cheese to the top, pour the milk over all, and sprinkle with remaining bran and the Cheddar cheese.
5. Bake uncovered at 350 degrees for 1 hour.

Italian Acorn Squash

❦

Serves 4
Bran per serving: 2 tablespoons

This hearty vegetable makes a colorful addition to a Thanksgiving dinner.

>   2 acorn squash
>   4 tablespoons soft margarine
>   ½ cup **bran**
>   1 (8-ounce) can tomato sauce
>   2 to 3 scallions, diced
>   Grated Parmesan cheese

1. Preheat oven to 350 degrees.
2. Boil squash for 1 hour in heavy cooking pot, then cut in halves, remove seeds, and place cut side up in a glass baking dish.
3. Place 1 tablespoon margarine in each half and sprinkle on 2 tablespoons bran per half.
4. Divide the tomato sauce among squash halves and top with scallions and Parmesan cheese.
5. Bake at 350 degrees for 15 to 20 minutes.

MICROWAVE METHOD:

1. Cut squash in half, remove seeds, and place cut side down in a glass baking dish. Cover with plastic wrap and microwave on high for 10 minutes.
2. Turn squash cut side up and add the rest of the ingredients, following directions above.
3. Cover with plastic wrap and microwave on high for 2 more minutes, or until heated through.

Crunchy-Top Tomatoes

🐦

Serves 4
Bran per serving: 1 teaspoon

These Italian-style tomatoes make a decorative vegetable accompaniment to any meal, and each serving
has 1 teaspoon of your daily required bran.

> 2 large firm ripe tomatoes, thickly sliced (½ inch)
> **Bran**
> Chopped fresh (or dried basil), to taste
> Minced garlic (or garlic powder), to taste
> Olive oil
> Grated Parmesan cheese, to taste

1. Preheat oven to broil (500 degrees).
2. Place thick tomato slices in a baking dish large
   enough to hold them easily.
3. On each tomato slice, sprinkle ½ teaspoon bran,
   add basil, garlic, a few drops of oil, and Parmesan
   cheese to taste, in that order.
4. Broil for 5 minutes until bubbly and crunchy.
   Serve immediately.

Stuffed Baby Tomatoes

❦
Serves 4
Bran per serving: 1 tablespoon

These little tomatoes make a good side dish for lunch, and they also work well as appetizers.

>1 pint cherry tomatoes, washed
>1 (6½-ounce) can water-packed tuna fish (or 2 small cans deviled ham)
>2 tablespoons light mayonnaise
>¼ cup **bran**
>2 tablespoons minced scallions (optional)
>Season to taste with: salt, pepper, garlic powder, and/or lemon pepper seasoning

1. Cut the cherry tomatoes in half and remove the center pulp with the smallest (⅛ teaspoon) measuring spoon.
2. Combine tuna, mayonnaise, bran, scallions, and seasonings.
3. Mix well and fill the tomato centers to heaping.
4. Refrigerate and serve chilled.

🍎 BREADS AND MUFFINS 🍎

Breads

Chocolate Zucchini Bread

❦ Makes 1 large loaf or 3 to 4 small loaves, 12 servings
Bran per serving: 1 tablespoon per slice

This bread is particularly moist and delicious.

    2 eggs (or 3 egg whites)
    1 cup brown sugar
    ½ cup light olive oil
    1 teaspoon vanilla extract
    2 tablespoons unsweetened cocoa
    1 cup grated zucchini
    1 cup whole wheat flour
    ¾ cup **bran**
    ½ teaspoon cinnamon
    1 teaspoon baking soda
    ¼ teaspoon baking powder
    ½ teaspoon salt
    1 cup chopped nuts (optional)

1. Preheat oven to 350 degrees. Have ready a greased 9 × 5-inch loaf pan or three 5 × 3-inch pans.
2. Cream together eggs, sugar, oil, vanilla extract, and cocoa.
3. Add grated zucchini and mix well.
4. Blend in remaining ingredients. Add nuts if desired.
5. Bake in prepared pan at 350 degrees for 60 to 70 minutes.
6. Allow to cool before cutting.

Old Fashioned Oatmeal Bread

❦   Makes 2 loaves, 24 slices
Bran per serving: ¾ cup per loaf; 1 tablespoon per slice

I don't usually spend the extra time to make yeast
breads, but every now and then my family craves this
wonderful old-fashioned bread—and it's full of bran,
oats, and other good things.

> 2 cups boiling water
> 1 cup dry rolled oats
> 2 tablespoons soft margarine (or light olive oil)
> 2 (¼-ounce) packages yeast
> ⅓ cup lukewarm water
> 2 teaspoons salt
> ½ cup honey
> 2½ cups whole wheat flour
> 2 cups **bran**

1. Pour boiling water over oats and margarine and
   let stand until thoroughly softened.
2. Dissolve yeast in ⅓ cup lukewarm water.
3. Add salt and honey to oat mixture and stir in
   yeast.
4. Combine the flour and the bran; add ¾ of this
   combination to the oat mixture. Knead all together and gradually add the rest of the flour and
   bran combination until thoroughly absorbed.
5. Knead the dough until smooth and elastic. Put
   dough into a greased bowl and turn once to
   grease surface.
6. Cover bowl with a towel and let rise until doubled.
7. Preheat oven to 350 degrees. Have ready 2
   greased 9 × 5-inch loaf pans.

8. Punch down with your fist and divide the dough in two.
9. Shape dough into 2 loaves and place in prepared loaf pans.
10. Allow dough to rise to top of pans.
11. Bake at 350 degrees for 50 minutes. Makes 2 loaves.

Applesauce-Raisin Bread

❦

Makes 1 loaf, 12 servings
Bran per slice: 1 tablespoon

If you can wait that long, this bread slices best the second day.

> 1 cup applesauce
> 1 egg
> ¼ cup soft margarine
> ½ cup brown sugar
> ½ cup **bran**
> 1½ cups whole wheat flour
> 2 teaspoons baking powder
> ½ teaspoon salt
> ½ teaspoon baking soda
> 1½ teaspoons cinnamon
> 1 teaspoon nutmeg
> 1 teaspoon ground cloves
> 1 teaspoon allspice
> 1 cup raisins

1. Preheat oven to 350 degrees. Have ready a greased 9 × 5-inch loaf pan.
2. Combine all ingredients and mix until smooth.
3. Turn into prepared pan.
4. Bake at 350 degrees for 1 hour.

Orange-Raisin Bread

Makes 1 large loaf or 3 to 4 small loaves, 12 servings
Bran per serving: 1 tablespoon

This bread is perfect for tea or afternoon snacking.

1 cup whole wheat flour
1 cup **bran**
1 teaspoon baking soda
1 cup buttermilk (or sour milk)
1 egg (or 2 egg whites)
1 (6-ounce) can orange juice concentrate
1 cup raisins

1. Preheat oven to 350 degrees. Have ready a greased 9 × 5-inch loaf pan.
2. Combine the dry ingredients.
3. Add the buttermilk or sour milk, egg, and orange juice concentrate and mix well. Blend in raisins.
4. Pour into prepared pan and bake at 350 degrees for 1 hour.

Pumpkin Bread

Makes 1 loaf or 3 to 4 small loaves, 12 servings
Bran per slice: 1 tablespoon

A favorite in the fall season. Serve this bread at your next Halloween party.

1½ cups whole wheat flour
½ cup **bran**
2 teaspoons baking powder
½ teaspoon salt
1 teaspoon cinnamon
½ teaspoon nutmeg
1 cup canned pumpkin
1 cup brown sugar
½ cup low-fat (1%) milk
2 eggs, beaten (or 3 egg whites)
¼ cup soft margarine (or light olive oil)
1 cup chopped pecans

1. Preheat oven to 350 degrees. Have ready a greased 9 × 5-inch loaf pan.
2. Mix together the dry ingredients in a large bowl.
3. Add the pumpkin, brown sugar, milk, eggs, and margarine or oil and mix until well blended.
4. Stir in nuts and turn into prepared pan.
5. Bake at 350 degrees for 50 to 55 minutes.
6. Cool before slicing.

Cranberry Bread

❦ Makes 1 large loaf or 3 to 4 small loaves, 12 servings
Bran per slice: 1 tablespoon

This bread is a great idea for the holidays.

1½ cups whole wheat flour
1 cup **bran**
1 cup brown sugar
2 teaspoons baking powder
½ teaspoon baking soda
1 teaspoon salt
½ cup orange juice
2 tablespoons light olive oil
1 (15-ounce) can jellied cranberries

1. Preheat oven to 350 degrees. Have ready a greased 9 × 5-inch loaf pan.
2. Combine the dry ingredients in a large bowl.
3. Add remaining ingredients and mix well.
4. Pour the batter into prepared pan.
5. Bake at 350 degrees for 50 to 60 minutes.

❧ USING OILS WITH BRAN

You'll notice that most of the recipes in this book call for soft margarine or light olive oil. These oils are particularly low in cholesterol, but they also happen to be the fats that blend most easily with bran. If you'd like the stronger flavor of regular olive oil in a particular dish, by all means use it.

Aunt Honey's Banana Bread

❦ Makes 1 large loaf or 3 to 4 small loaves, 12 servings
Bran per slice: 1 tablespoon

My aunt Honey gave me this recipe soon after I was married and it has worked beautifully in several states and two foreign countries. With bran added, it's healthful and delicious.

> ½ cup soft margarine (or light olive oil)
> 1 cup brown sugar
> 2 eggs, beaten (or 3 egg whites)
> 1½ cups whole wheat flour
> 1 teaspoon baking soda
> ½ cup **bran**
> ½ teaspoon salt
> 2 to 3 ripe bananas, mashed
> ½ cup chopped nuts (optional)

1. Preheat oven to 350 degrees.
2. Cream shortening and sugar; add eggs and beat well.
3. Add flour, baking soda, bran, and salt.
4. Add mashed bananas and nuts, if using them. Mix well.
5. Bake in three 5 × 3-inch loaf pans or one 9 × 5-inch loaf pan. Line the pans with a generous piece of aluminum foil, then fill with batter and bake as usual. This is not only easy, there is also no mess.
6. Bake at 350 degrees for 1 hour.

Strawberry Bread

❦ Makes 1 large loaf or 3 to 4 small loaves, 12 servings
Bran per slice: 1 tablespoon

Strawberry bread is delicious with coffee or tea. It's also perfect for breakfast.

¾ cup whole wheat flour
¾ cup **bran**
1 teaspoon baking soda
½ teaspoon salt
1 teaspoon cinnamon
1 cup brown sugar
2 eggs (or 3 egg whites)
½ cup light olive oil
1 cup frozen sliced strawberries, thawed

1. Preheat oven to 350 degrees.
2. Combine all ingredients and mix well.
3. Pour into one 9 × 5-inch loaf pan or three 5 × 3-inch loaf pans. Line your pans with a generous piece of aluminum foil, then fill with batter and bake as usual for an easy cleanup.
4. Bake at 350 degrees for 60 to 70 minutes. Remove from oven and allow to cool, then remove from pans.

Cinnamon Rolls

❧

Makes 12 rolls
Bran per roll: 1 tablespoon

These are a bit of a fuss but they're absolutely worth it. They can be frosted with a mixture of 1 cup powdered sugar and 1½ tablespoons milk. Mix until smooth and drizzle on rolls.

DOUGH

¼ cup brown sugar
1 teaspoon salt
2 cups whole wheat flour
1 (¼-ounce) package quick-rising yeast
1 cup **bran**
¾ cup low-fat (1%) milk
¾ cup water
4 tablespoons soft margarine (or light olive oil)
1 egg, beaten (or 2 egg whites)

FILLING

2 tablespoons soft margarine
¾ to 1 cup brown sugar
Raisins (optional)
Cinnamon, to taste
Margarine

1. Preheat oven to 375 degrees. Have ready a greased 9 × 12-inch baking pan.
2. Combine sugar, salt, flour, yeast, and bran in a large mixing bowl.
3. Heat milk, water, and margarine or oil in a 1-quart saucepan over medium heat.

4. Stir milk mixture into dry ingredients.
5. Add egg and mix to a soft dough, adding more flour to make smooth if the mixture is sticky.
6. Knead 8 to 10 minutes on lightly floured surface.
7. Place in greased bowl and allow to rise, greased side up, until double in size, about 35 minutes.
8. Punch down and roll into rectangle about 14×8 inches.

To make the filling:

9. Melt 2 tablespoons margarine and spread on dough.
10. Spread on brown sugar and raisins (if desired) and sprinkle with cinnamon, to taste.
11. Roll up lengthwise, cut into 12 pieces, and place in prepared baking pan. Cover and let rise until double, about 30 minutes.
12. Dot with margarine and bake at 375 degrees for 20 to 25 minutes. Turn out of pan onto cooling rack when done.

❧ THE IMPORTANCE OF DRINKING WATER

All of us know that drinking a lot of water is an easy way to improve our health. But when you're on a bran regime, it's particularly important to add a glass of water for each tablespoon of bran in addition to the six glasses you should be drinking anyway. Three more glasses of water a day will do the trick.

Southern Corn Bread

❧

Serves 4
Bran per slice: 2 tablespoons

For dinner, slice corn bread squares in half and serve with syrup or honey. Serve the leftover corn bread this same way for breakfast the next day.

> 1 cup cornmeal
> ½ cup **bran**
> ½ cup whole wheat flour
> 1 teaspoon salt
> 1 cup buttermilk (or sour milk)
> 2 teaspoons baking powder
> 1 egg, beaten (or 2 egg whites)
> ⅓ cup light olive oil
> 3 tablespoons molasses (or honey)

1. Preheat oven to 375 degrees. Have ready a greased 8 × 8-inch or 9 × 5-inch pan.
2. Mix all ingredients together well.
3. Pour batter into pan and bake at 375 degrees for 25 to 30 minutes.
4. Serve warm.

❧ BREAD BAKING MADE EASY

If you'd like to forget about greasing the bread pans and cleaning them up later, just line the pan with a length of aluminum foil and pour the batter right in. If you leave some extra foil, you can just let the baked bread cool in the foil, then wrap it up tightly for storage or freezing.

Muffins

Raisin and Bran Muffins

❦
Makes 12 muffins
Bran per muffin: 2 tablespoons

These muffins can be mixed ahead and the batter kept in the refrigerator for at least a month. When you're ready to bake, simply start at step 4.

> 1½ cups whole wheat flour
> 1½ cups **bran**
> 2 cups low-fat (1%) milk
> 1 cup molasses
> ½ cup brown sugar
> 2 tablespoons soft margarine (or light olive oil)
> 1 egg (or 2 egg whites)
> 1¼ teaspoons baking soda
> ¼ teaspoon salt
> ½ to 1 cup raisins

1. Preheat oven to 400 degrees. Have ready a greased 12-cup muffin tin.
2. Mix flour, bran, and milk slowly.
3. Add remaining ingredients and mix well.
4. Drop mixture into prepared muffin cups to their tops.
5. Bake at 400 degrees for 25 to 30 minutes. Remove from oven and allow to cool 5 to 10 minutes.

Quick Bran Muffins

Makes 12 muffins
Bran per muffin: 2 teaspoons

Make these muffins ahead of time and freeze them. Defrost them for a bran treat at any time of the day.

    1 (16-ounce) package nut bread or date bread mix
    ½ cup **bran**
    2 eggs (or 3 egg whites)
    ¼ cup water
    1 teaspoon fresh lemon juice
    1 cup chopped nuts
    1 cup raisins

1. Preheat oven to 350 degrees. Have ready a greased muffin tin.
2. In a large bowl, combine all ingredients and mix well.
3. Fill prepared muffin cups, ¾ full.
4. Bake at 350 degrees for 25 minutes. Serve warm.

Applesauce-Oat Muffins

Makes 12 muffins
Bran per muffin: 2 teaspoons

These muffins are easy to put together and are great with soup or salad for dinner. They also make good breakfast muffins.

½ cup whole wheat flour
½ cup **bran**
1 cup quick-cooking oats
1 teaspoon baking soda
1 teaspoon baking powder
1 teaspoon cinnamon
1 cup applesauce
3 tablespoons light olive oil
¼ cup molasses
1 egg

1. Preheat oven to 350 degrees. Have ready a greased muffin tin.
2. Combine all ingredients and mix well.
3. Spoon batter into prepared muffin cups.
4. Bake at 350 degrees for 20 minutes.

Carrot-Cake Muffins

❦

Makes 12 muffins
Bran per muffin: 2 teaspoons

These muffins are an updated (with bran) version of
an old favorite. They make a good breakfast muffin,
but they're also good for dessert.

½ cup whole wheat flour
½ cup **bran**
1 cup quick-cooking oats
3 teaspoons baking powder
½ teaspoon salt
3 teaspoons brown sugar
2 eggs (or 3 egg whites)
¼ cup light olive oil
1 cup buttermilk (or sour milk)
⅔ cup finely grated carrots

1. Preheat oven to 400 degrees. Have ready a greased
   muffin tin.
2. Combine the flour, bran, oats, baking powder,
   salt, and sugar.
3. Beat together the eggs, oil, and buttermilk; add to
   flour combination.
4. Add grated carrots and mix until moistened.
5. Spoon mixture into prepared muffin cups.
6. Bake at 400 degrees about 20 to 25 minutes.

ICING

1 (3-ounce) package cream cheese
½ stick (¼ cup) margarine
½ (10-ounce) package powdered sugar
1 teaspoon vanilla extract
Low-fat (1%) milk

1. Cream all ingredients together, adding milk a teaspoon at a time until spreadable.
2. Spread icing on cooled muffins.

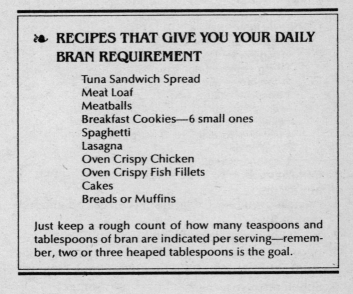

❧ RECIPES THAT GIVE YOU YOUR DAILY BRAN REQUIREMENT

Tuna Sandwich Spread
Meat Loaf
Meatballs
Breakfast Cookies—6 small ones
Spaghetti
Lasagna
Oven Crispy Chicken
Oven Crispy Fish Fillets
Cakes
Breads or Muffins

Just keep a rough count of how many teaspoons and tablespoons of bran are indicated per serving—remember, two or three heaped tablespoons is the goal.

Banana-Date Muffins

❧

Makes 12 muffins
Bran per muffin: 1 tablespoon

These sweet, moist muffins are good with coffee for a mid-morning break. If you don't like dates, substitute raisins.

> 1 cup **bran**
> 1 cup whole wheat flour
> ¼ cup low-fat (1%) milk
> 1⅓ cups mashed ripe bananas
> ¼ cup brown sugar
> 1 teaspoon baking soda
> ½ teaspoon salt
> 2 eggs (or 3 egg whites)
> 4 tablespoons melted soft margarine (or light olive oil)
> 1 teaspoon vanilla extract
> ½ cup chopped dates (or raisins)

1. Preheat oven to 400 degrees. Have ready a greased muffin tin.
2. Mix all ingredients and blend well.
3. Spoon batter into prepared muffin cups and bake 20 to 30 minutes at 400 degrees, until tops are golden.

Poppy Seed Muffins

❧

Makes 12 muffins
Bran per muffin: 1 tablespoon

These muffins are simply wonderful. You can also brush them with a glaze of lemon juice and powdered sugar if you'd like to dress them up a little.

¾ cup soft margarine (or light olive oil)
1 cup brown sugar
2 eggs, beaten (or 3 egg whites)
Grated peel of 1 lemon (optional)
¼ cup lemon juice (or juice of ½ lemon)
1½ teaspoons vanilla extract
½ teaspoon baking soda
½ teaspoon salt
1¼ cups buttermilk (or sour milk)
1½ cups whole wheat flour
1 cup **bran**
½ cup poppy seeds

1. Preheat oven to 375 degrees. Have ready a greased muffin tin.
2. Cream margarine, sugar, and eggs together. Add peel (if desired), lemon juice, and vanilla extract.
3. Add baking soda, salt, and buttermilk. Blend well.
4. Add dry ingredients and mix thoroughly.
5. Fill prepared muffin cups with mixture.
6. Bake at 375 degrees for 20 minutes, or until browned on top.

Strawberry-Yogurt Muffins

❦

Makes 12 muffins
Bran per muffin: 1 tablespoon

These moist, delicious muffins are particularly good
with fruit salad.

> 1 cup whole wheat flour
> 1 cup **bran**
> ½ cup brown sugar
> 1½ teaspoons baking soda
> ½ teaspoon salt
> 2 eggs (or 3 egg whites)
> 1 cup plain low-fat yogurt
> 1 teaspoon vanilla extract
> 1 tablespoon soft margarine (or light olive oil)
> 1 cup fresh strawberries mashed with 2
>   tablespoons of sugar (or 1 cup thawed,
>   frozen, sliced strawberries)

1. Preheat oven to 375 degrees. Have ready a greased
   muffin tin.
2. Combine flour, bran, sugar, baking soda, and salt.
3. Add eggs, yogurt, vanilla extract, margarine, and
   strawberries to flour mixture and blend.
4. Spoon mixture into prepared muffin cups.
5. Bake 30 to 40 minutes at 375 degrees, or until tops
   are golden.

❧ SANDWICHES AND SPREADS ❧

Spreads

Egg Salad Spread

❦

Serves 4
Bran per serving: 1 to 1½ teaspoons

Children love this spread for sandwiches that they can make themselves, and it's a healthful way to use up all of your Easter eggs—unless you have high cholesterol, of course.

6 hard-cooked eggs, peeled
2 tablespoons **bran,** to taste
2 to 3 tablespoons light mayonnaise
2 celery stalks, diced
2 to 3 scallions, diced (optional)
Salt and pepper, to taste

1. Mash eggs and combine with bran.
2. Add remaining ingredients and blend well.

❧ HOW MUCH BRAN DO YOU NEED?

Most people need two to three heaped tablespoons a day, or about thirty to forty grams. Most breakfast cereals have five to nine grams, ten at the most, so you can see why you need to supplement your breakfast cereal. Overloading on bran will cause cramping and possibly constipation for a day. If that happens, back off and drink more water; the problem will solve itself in a day or two, and you can slowly add more bran to your diet.

Salmon Salad Spread

❧

Serves 4
Bran per serving: 2 teaspoons

Here we have a salad in a sandwich, plus bran. So you have protein, vegetables, and fiber all in one.

1 (6½-ounce) can pink salmon, undrained
¼ cup **bran**
¼ cup light mayonnaise
½ cup minced scallions
½ cup minced celery
½ cup minced dill pickle
½ cup minced radishes (optional)
2 garlic cloves, minced (or 1 teaspoon garlic powder)
1 teaspoon lemon pepper seasoning

Mix ingredients together until well blended.

❧ ADDING BRAN TO YOUR DIET

Remember to start slowly when you're getting your system accustomed to bran. Start with a teaspoon a day, then build up to two to three heaped tablespoons. The goal is to maintain the bran input—once your body's used to this regime, you'll feel so good you won't be likely to forget your bran. But if you start with too much too soon, you won't forget that experience either. Always introduce bran mixed into food to avoid explosive digestive problems.

Tuna Sandwich Spread

❦

Serves 4
Bran per serving: 1 to 2 tablespoons

Dr. Jewell says the bran-tuna sandwich mixture separates the men from the boys—the men mix the ½ cup bran in and love it. This spread is an easy way to get your necessary bran fiber for the day in one swoop.

> 1 (6½-ounce) can water-packed tuna fish
> ¼ to ½ cup **bran**
> ¼ to ½ cup light mayonnaise (use more with
>   increased bran amount)
> Salt, pepper, lemon pepper seasoning, or garlic
>   powder, to taste

Mix all ingredients together well.

ADDITIONS TO TUNA SANDWICH SPREAD
MIXTURE:

> ½ cup chopped radishes
> ½ cup minced scallions
> ½ cup minced celery

Liver Pâté Spread

❦

Serves 4
Bran per serving: 2 tablespoons

This tasty spread is the one sure way I know to get children to eat liver, so you know it's delicious.

½ pound liverwurst
½ cup **bran**
½ cup plain low-fat yogurt
¼ cup light mayonnaise
1 tablespoon Worcestershire sauce
½ cup diced celery
½ cup diced scallions (optional)

Mix ingredients together and beat until very smooth.

Sandwiches

Pocket Sandwiches

❦

Serves 6
Bran per serving: 4 teaspoons

½ to 1 pound lean ground beef or ground turkey
½ cup **bran**
Salt and pepper, to taste
1 (1½-ounce) package gravy mix (or make Bran-
    New Gravy, page 228)
1½ cups water
6 to 8 pita breads, cut in half

1. Brown the meat and the bran together over medium heat in a heatproof serving dish.

2. Season to taste and add the gravy mix and the water; mix well.
3. Spoon filling into pita bread pockets and add toppings:

TOPPINGS:

Chopped lettuce
Chopped onion
Chopped radish
Grated cheese

No-Meat Pocket Sandwiches

❦

Serves 4
Bran per serving: ½ to 1 tablespoon

These sandwiches taste "meaty" and satisfying, but they don't contain any meat. They're a good choice when you want a hearty sandwich but you're not in the mood for meat.

1 recipe Bran-New Gravy (see next recipe) (or 1
    package gravy mix plus ¼ cup **bran** and ½ to
    1 cups water)
2 cooked medium potatoes, diced
½ cup diced scallions (optional)
4 pita breads, cut in half

1. Prepare gravy in a heatproof serving dish.
2. Add diced potatoes and scallions and mix well.
3. Spoon filling into pita bread pockets and serve with the same toppings as in the previous pocket sandwich recipe.

Bran-New Gravy

❦

Serves 4
Bran per serving: ½ tablespoon

Commercial gravy mixes can be made into bran gravy by adding ¼ cup of bran plus an extra ½ to 1 cup of water to any packaged gravy mix. Or try this home-made easy bran gravy, which has all sorts of kitchen uses.

1 cup water
⅛ cup **bran**
⅛ cup flour
1 to 2 teaspoons instant low-sodium beef (or
    chicken) bouillon
¼ to ½ cup drippings from cooked meat—
    chicken, turkey, roast beef or pork, pork
    chops, meat loaf, etc.
Salt and pepper, to taste

1. Mix the water, bran, flour, and instant bouillon together well until smooth.
2. Slowly add the thickening to warm drippings in a saucepan over medium heat.
3. Add an additional 2 to 3 cups or more water, until gravy is the right consistency.
4. Stir continuously for several minutes and season to taste.

Sloppy Joes

❧

Serves 4
Bran per serving: 2 tablespoons

This recipe absolutely disguises bran, so this is a good place to start your family on their healthful new life-style.

> ½ pound lean ground beef (or ground turkey)
> ½ cup **bran**
> 1 to 2 tablespoons olive oil, if necessary
> 1 (8-ounce) can tomato sauce
> 1 (15-ounce) can kidney beans (optional)
> 2 garlic cloves, minced (or 1 teaspoon garlic powder)
> ¼ teaspoon pepper
> Hamburger buns

1. In a skillet over medium heat, brown meat and bran together, using oil if necessary.
2. Add the tomato sauce and beans.
3. Simmer on low heat until heated through.
4. Spoon onto hamburger buns.

Sloppy Dogs

❦

Serves 4
Bran per serving: 2 tablespoons

This recipe was invented because I had hot dog buns and no hot dogs; it works just as well on hard rolls.

> ½ pound lean ground beef (or ground turkey)
> ½ cup **bran**
> 1 (8-ounce) can tomato sauce
> Grated Cheddar cheese
> Diced scallions (optional)
> 4 hot dog buns or hard rolls, split

1. In a skillet over medium heat, brown the ground meat and bran together.
2. Add the tomato sauce and simmer 20 minutes.
3. To serve, spoon over hot dog buns or into centers of hard rolls and top with grated cheese and scallions.

❧ NO-STICK COOKING SPRAY

This very useful product is sold under various trade names, such as Pam. It has no sodium, no cholesterol, and it's low-fat and low-calorie in comparison to margarine and other oils you'd use instead. Best of all, it's very easy to use.

Grilled Bran-Burgers

❦

Serves 6
Bran per serving: 1 tablespoon

Burgers can absorb a lot of bran, and no one will be the wiser. You can also use much less meat if you're adding bran, so it's economical as well as healthful.

> ½ cup **bran**
> Salt, pepper, garlic powder, or other seasonings, to taste
> 1 pound lean ground beef (or ground turkey)
> 6 hamburger buns

1. Mix bran and desired seasonings into ground meat.
2. Shape into patties and grill or broil.

Tip: If you forget to add bran to hamburgers, or if you are using premolded hamburger patties, try this trick: sprinkle each patty with about ½ teaspoon bran before you cook the meat. The burgers will be crispy on the outside.

Denver-Hash Sandwich Spread

❦

Serves 8
Bran per serving: 1 tablespoon

This is a substantial sandwich spread. It will absorb a lot of bran. My family likes to add slices of dill pickle to the sandwiches.

> 1 (15-ounce) can corned beef hash
> ½ cup **bran** or more, to taste
> 1 cup diced celery
> ½ cup diced scallions
> ½ cup diced green pepper
> 2 tablespoons Worcestershire sauce
> 2 garlic cloves, minced (or 1 teaspoon garlic powder)
> 2 dashes of Tabasco (optional)
> 2 eggs, beaten (or 3 egg whites)
> ¼ cup low-fat (1%) milk

1. Combine the hash, bran, vegetables, and seasonings together in a skillet over medium heat and simmer 20 to 30 minutes.
2. Beat together the egg and milk and mix into hash.
3. Simmer mixture for 5 to 10 minutes more, until egg has cooked. Serve on toast.

Lemon Bars

❦

Serves 6
Bran per serving: 2 teaspoons

These lemon bars make their own crust. If you like an intensely lemony taste, add a teaspoon of grated lemon peel along with the juice.

> ¼ cup brown sugar
> ⅓ cup soft margarine
> 1 egg (or 2 egg whites)
> ¼ cup **bran**
> ½ cup whole wheat flour
> 3 eggs (or 4 egg whites)
> ½ cup brown sugar
> ⅓ cup fresh lemon juice
> ½ cup additional soft margarine
> Low-fat whipped cream topping

1. Preheat oven to 375 degrees.
2. Combine the sugar, margarine, and egg and beat until smooth.
3. Add the bran and flour, mix well, and press into an 8 × 8-inch baking pan.
4. Beat together the remaining ingredients and pour onto the bran crust.
5. Bake at 375 degrees for 30 to 40 minutes. Cool before cutting, and serve with low-fat whipped cream and/or sliced bananas on top.

Rice Krispies Bars

❦

Makes 12 bars
Bran per bar: 2 teaspoons

I wouldn't have thought of putting bran into Rice Krispies bars—or even *making* Rice Krispies bars, for that matter—but one day my daughter Tiffany wanted to make some to send to her brother. I was less than enthusiastic, but when she offered to put bran in them, I said yes. It was a big success—her brother and his friends made short work of them, and he was amazed to learn later that they had bran in them.

> ¼ cup soft margarine
> 30 marshmallows
> ½ cup **bran**
> 5 cups Kellogg's Rice Krispies

1. Melt margarine in a large saucepan over low heat.
2. Add marshmallows and stir until completely melted.
3. Remove from heat; add bran and Rice Krispies. Stir together until completely coated.
4. Pour into a greased 9 × 13-inch pan, using a spatula or wax paper to press mixture evenly into pan.
5. Allow to cool and cut into 12 equal bars.

Heavenly Brownies

❦

Serves 6
Bran per brownie: 4 teaspoons

These delectable brownies are very rich and so good that it's hard to believe they could be good for you—but they are.

> ⅓ cup light olive oil
> 1 cup brown sugar
> 2 eggs (or 3 egg whites)
> ½ cup **bran**
> ¼ cup whole wheat flour
> 1 teaspoon baking powder
> ½ teaspoon salt
> 2 tablespoons unsweetened cocoa
> ½ cup chopped nuts (optional)

1. Preheat oven to 350 degrees. Have ready a greased 8 × 8-inch or 9 × 12-inch baking pan.
2. Combine all ingredients and mix well; mixture will be thick, so mix slowly.
3. Fold mixture into prepared pan.
4. Bake at 350 for 25 minutes. Do not overbake.

Strawberry Shortcake

❧

Serves 8
Bran per serving: 1 tablespoon

Everyone loves strawberry shortcake, even in winter. This one has lots of bran, and it's every bit as delicious as the classic one.

> 1 quart fresh strawberries, cleaned and sliced, or
>   3 (10-ounce packages) frozen sliced
>   strawberries, thawed
> ½ cup brown sugar
> 1½ cups whole wheat flour
> ½ cup **bran**
> 3 teaspoons baking powder
> 1 teaspoon salt
> ⅓ cup soft margarine (or light olive oil)
> 1 cup low-fat (1%) milk
> 1 teaspoon vanilla extract
> Low-fat whipped cream topping

1. Preheat oven to 400 degrees. Have ready 2 greased 8-inch layer cake pans.
2. If using fresh berries, add a little sugar and allow to stand at room temperature for 1 hour.
3. Combine all dry ingredients in large mixing bowl.
4. Blend in margarine or oil, and add milk and vanilla extract.
5. Pour batter into prepared cake pans.
6. Bake at 400 degrees for 15 to 20 minutes.
7. Remove from oven, allow to cool, and remove from pans.

8. Place one layer cake on serving plate and cover with strawberries. Top with remaining layer cake and cover with remaining berries.
9. Top with low-fat whipped cream topping and serve.

❧ REPLACING WHOLE EGGS WITH EGG WHITES

If you'd like to avoid the extra cholesterol in eggs when you're baking, you can simply use egg whites, which will work in nearly all cases. For recipes in this book, I've indicated the quantities. To convert your own recipes, use this formula:

    3 eggs = 4 egg whites
    2 eggs = 3 egg whites
    1 egg = 2 egg whites

Cupcakes

❦

Makes 12 cupcakes
Bran per cupcake: 2 teaspoons

These very easy cupcakes have only 1 egg—or no egg
yolks, if cholesterol is a problem. Bake them in paper
cupcake holders for an easy cleanup.

> 1½ cups whole wheat flour
> ½ cup **bran**
> 1 cup brown sugar
> 2½ teaspoons baking powder
> 1 teaspoon salt
> ⅓ cup soft margarine (or light olive oil)
> 1 cup low-fat (1%) milk
> 1 teaspoon vanilla extract
> 1 egg (or 2 egg whites)

1. Preheat oven to 350 degrees.
2. Combine all ingredients and mix well.
3. Spoon mixture into paper cupcake holders and/or
   greased muffin tin.
4. Bake at 350 degrees for 25 to 30 minutes.

VARIATIONS:

> Chocolate cupcakes: add ¼ cup unsweetened
>   cocoa
> Spice cupcakes: add ½ teaspoon cinnamon
>   add ¼ teaspoon each ground cloves,
>   allspice, and nutmeg

Susan's Apple Brown Betty

❦

Serves 6
Bran per serving: 2 teaspoons

This is my friend Susan's recipe with bran added. For my taste, it's one of the best desserts in this life.

TOPPING:

½ cup soft margarine
½ to ¾ cup brown sugar
¼ cup whole wheat flour
¼ cup **bran**
1 teaspoon cinnamon

5 to 6 cups apples, washed, peeled, and sliced
Nonfat whipped topping

1. Preheat oven to 375 degrees.
2. Combine the topping ingredients, mixing well and mashing together.
3. Place the apples in a greased 9 × 12-inch baking dish and cover with the topping.
4. Bake 45 minutes at 375 degrees.
5. Allow to cool and serve with nonfat whipped topping.

Apricot Upside-Down Cake

❧

Serves 12
Bran per serving: 1 teaspoon

If you like upside-down cakes, try this one. It's
especially nice in winter, when apricots seem to spell
sunshine.

> ⅔ cup brown sugar
> 3 tablespoons soft margarine
> 1 tablespoon water
> ½ cup **bran**
> 1 (16-ounce) can unpeeled apricot halves, drained
>   (save juice)
> ⅓ cup additional soft margarine (or light olive oil)
> ¾ cup brown sugar
> 1 egg (or 2 egg whites)
> 1½ teaspoons vanilla extract
> 1¼ cups whole wheat flour
> 2½ teaspoons baking powder
> ½ teaspoon salt
> 1 cup drained apricot juice plus milk

1. Preheat oven to 350 degrees.
2. Combine sugar, margarine, and water; spread in a
   9 × 9-inch baking pan.
3. Sprinkle with ¼ cup bran and arrange apricot
   halves on top.
4. Mix together the remaining ingredients, including
   the drained apricot juice plus enough milk to make
   1 cup and the remaining ¼ cup bran.
5. Spread cake batter over the apricot layer.
6. Bake in a 350-degree oven for 35 to 40 minutes.
   Slice the cake in squares so that each piece has its
   own apricot filling.

Easy Apple-Cinnamon Cake

❦

Serves 8
Bran per serving: 1 tablespoon

This is the easiest cake you'll ever make . . . period.

> 4 tablespoons soft margarine, melted
> 1 cup brown sugar
> 1 egg (or 2 egg whites)
> 1 teaspoon baking soda
> ½ teaspoon salt
> 1 teaspoon cinnamon
> 1½ cups diced apples (about 2 to 3 apples)
> ½ cup whole wheat flour
> ½ cup **bran**

1. Preheat oven to 300 degrees. Have ready a greased 9 × 9-inch baking pan.
2. Combine the margarine, sugar, egg, baking soda, salt, and cinnamon. Add apples and mix well.
3. Stir in flour and bran. Fold into prepared pan.
4. Bake at 300 degrees for 1 hour. Serve warm.

❧ GUESSING THE FAT CONTENT OF COOKIES AND CAKES

A popular rule of thumb that's appeared frequently in the press is that soft cookies and moist cakes—usually our favorites—are the ones to stay away from, because they have the highest fat content. If you're using bran, though, this rule is all wrong. Because the bran fiber holds the moisture in, you can have moist baked goods without worrying about higher fat levels.

Pumpkin Pie

❧
Serves 6
Bran per serving: 2 teaspoons

This is a delicious no-fail pie that makes its own crust while it cooks.

> 1 (16-ounce) can cooked pumpkin
> 1 (14-ounce) can sweetened condensed milk
> 1 egg (or 2 egg whites)
> ¼ cup Bisquick
> ¼ cup **bran**
> ¼ teaspoon ground cloves
> 1 teaspoon ground cinnamon
> Low-fat whipped cream topping
> No-stick cooking spray

1. Preheat oven to 350 degrees. Have ready a 9-inch pie plate that has been sprayed with cooking spray.
2. Combine ingredients in a blender or food processor and blend for 1 minute, or beat for 2 minutes with mixer in a mixing bowl.
3. Pour into prepared pie plate.
4. Bake at 350 degrees for 50 minutes.
5. Allow to cool, and serve with a low-fat whipped cream topping.

Graham Cracker Pie Crust

🍒

Serves 8
Bran per serving: 1½ teaspoons

You can use your favorite recipe with this crust, or any packaged pudding and pie filling; the sugarless ones make a guilt-free dessert. But even if you go whole hog, at least you're getting some bran with your calories.

> 1 cup graham cracker crumbs
> ¼ cup **bran**
> 2 to 3 tablespoons brown sugar
> ¼ cup soft margarine

1. Preheat oven to 350 degrees.
2. Mix all ingredients together.
3. Press mixture firmly and evenly into pie pan.
4. Bake 10 minutes at 350 degrees.
5. Allow to cool and fill with any cream or chiffon pie filling.
6. Refrigerate at least one hour before serving.

Fresh Banana-Orange Cake

❦

Serves 9
Bran per serving: 2 teaspoons or more

Most of us keep bananas and oranges on hand in the
winter months, and all the other ingredients for this
small cake will already be in your pantry—so it's a
nice, fresh, spur-of-the-moment cake.

> 1 teaspoon finely grated orange peel
> 1 large ripe banana (or 2 small ripe bananas)
> ¼ cup soft margarine (or light olive oil)
> ⅔ cup brown sugar
> 1 egg, beaten (or 2 egg whites)
> 1 tablespoon orange juice
> ½ cup whole wheat flour
> ½ cup **bran**
> 1 teaspoon baking soda
> 1 teaspoon salt
> ½ to ¾ cup powdered sugar
> 2 teaspoons additional orange juice

1. Preheat oven to 350 degrees. Grate the orange
   peel. Have ready a greased 8 × 8-inch cake pan.
2. Cream together the banana, margarine, sugar,
   egg, orange juice, and orange peel.
3. Blend in the dry ingredients except the powdered
   sugar and mix well.
4. Pour into cake pan.
5. Bake at 350 degrees for 30 minutes. Cool in pan.
6. Make a glaze by mixing powdered sugar and orange juice; pour over cake.

Instant Gratification Chocolate Blender Cake

❦

Serves 9
Bran per serving: 2 teaspoons or more

When you just *have* to have a chocolate cake, this one is very fast and very chocolaty.

    1 cup cold water
    1 cup brown sugar
    1 egg
    3 tablespoons unsweetened cocoa
    ½ teaspoon salt
    ¼ cup light olive oil
    1 teaspoon vanilla extract
    1 tablespoon vinegar
    1 cup whole wheat flour
    ½ cup **bran**
    1 teaspoon baking soda

1. Preheat oven to 350 degrees. Have ready a greased 8 × 8-inch baking dish.
2. Combine all ingredients in blender and mix well.
3. Pour into prepared dish.
4. Bake at 350 degrees for 35 to 40 minutes.

Chocolate Cake

❦
Serves 12
Bran per serving: 2 teaspoons

This very good cake *never* fails, and it hides a lot of bran too.

> ¼ cup soft margarine (or light olive oil)
> ½ cup brown sugar
> 1 egg (or 2 egg whites)
> 2 tablespoons unsweetened cocoa
> ⅔ cup low-fat (1%) milk
> ⅓ cup buttermilk (or 1 cup sour milk)
> 1¼ cups whole wheat flour
> ½ cup **bran**
> ½ teaspoon baking soda
> ¼ teaspoon salt

1. Preheat oven to 350 degrees. Have ready a greased 9 × 12-inch glass baking dish.
2. Combine margarine, sugar, egg, and cocoa, and blend well.
3. Add milk and the remaining ingredients.
4. Blend until smooth and pour into prepared pan.
5. Bake at 350 degrees for 25 to 30 minutes.

Oatmeal Cake

❦

Serves 12
Bran per serving: 2 teaspoons

This substantial cake is great for snacks or breakfast—with oats *and* bran, it's healthful too.

This is a thick cake so it may take longer at some altitudes. It's also hearty and delicious, great for after-school snacks.

    1 cup quick-cooking oats
    1¼ cups boiling water
    1 cup brown sugar
    ½ cup molasses
    2 eggs (or 3 egg whites)
    ½ teaspoon salt
    1 teaspoon baking soda
    ½ cup soft margarine (or light olive oil)
    ½ cup **bran**
    1 cup whole wheat flour
    1 teaspoon vanilla extract
    1 teaspoon cinnamon

1. Combine the oats and boiling water and let stand 5 minutes.
2. Preheat oven to 350 degrees. Have ready a greased 9 × 12-inch baking pan.
3. Add the rest of the ingredients to the oatmeal mixture.
4. Blend well and turn into the prepared pan.
5. Bake at 350 degrees for 30 minutes, or until done when tested with a toothpick.

Oat Lace Cookies

❦

Makes 5 dozen
Bran per cookie: ¼ tablespoon

These delicate cookies are elegant enough to serve company for dessert. They're eggless, full of bran, and absolutely delicious. If you're just starting to use bran, they're a perfect introduction.

> ½ cup soft margarine, melted
> 1 cup brown sugar
> 1 cup quick-cooking oats
> 1 cup **bran**
> 2 tablespoons low-fat (1%) milk

1. Preheat oven to 350 degrees. Have ready a lightly greased cookie sheet.
2. Combine melted margarine and sugar.
3. Add the oats, bran, and milk; mix well.
4. Drop by teaspoonfuls or walnut-size balls onto prepared cookie sheet. Allow for a 3-inch spread on all sides of each cookie.
5. Bake at 350 degrees for 10 to 12 minutes. Do not overbake.
6. Allow to cool for 1 minute before removing from sheet.

Chocolate Fudge Pie

❦

Serves 6
Bran per serving: 1 teaspoon

This very easy dessert is like fudge in a pie—and it makes its own crust. Slice it very thinly, since it's quite rich. It's great with coffee.

>   3 eggs, beaten (or 4 egg whites, whipped)
>   ½ cup unsweetened cocoa
>   1 cup brown sugar
>   2 tablespoons **bran**
>   ½ teaspoon vanilla extract
>   ½ cup soft margarine, melted
>   1 cup chopped nuts
>   Whipped cream, any kind

1. Preheat oven to 350 degrees. Have ready a greased 9-inch pie plate.
2. Mix eggs, cocoa, sugar, bran, and vanilla extract.
3. Add melted margarine and nuts to egg mixture, and blend together well.
4. Pour into prepared pie plate and bake at 350 degrees for 30 minutes.
5. Top pie or each individual serving with whipped cream.

&. CONVERTING PACKAGED MIXES FOR BRAN-HEALTHFUL BAKING

Add ¼ to ½ cup bran, to taste, plus ¼ to ½ cup water or low-fat (1%) milk. This formula will work for cakes, breads, muffins, etc. Prepare and bake as directed by manufacturer. Here's a sample cake mix recipe, just to give you an idea of how easy it is.

Cake Mix Sample Recipe

Serves 8
Bran per serving: 1 tablespoon

This rich cake is living proof that bran can taste good.

> 1 (1-pound) 2½-ounce package pineapple cake
>   mix
> 1 (4-ounce) package instant vanilla pudding
> ½ cup **bran**
> ½ cup water
> 1 (17-ounce) can crushed pineapple, drained (save
>   juice)
> 1 (8-ounce) package vanilla frosting mix,
>   prepared (or 1 (12-ounce) can prepared
>   vanilla frosting)

1. Preheat oven as directed on cake mix package.
2. Prepare cake mix as directed on package.
3. Add pudding mix, bran, and additional water to cake mixture. Blend well.
4. Place mixture in a 9 × 12-inch baking pan and bake as directed on cake mix package.
5. When cake is baked, drain pineapple juice, drizzle juice on cake while still hot, and let cake cool.
6. Ice cake with frosting, and spread crushed pineapple on top.

Selected References

Anderson, J. W., and N. J. Gustafson. "Type II Diabetes: Current Nutrition Management Concepts." *Geriatrics*, 41, No. 8 (August 1986): 28–35.

Anderson, J. W., R. W. Kirby, and E. D. Rees. "Oat-Bran Selectively Lowers Serum Low-Density Lipoprotein Cholesterol Concentrations in Men." *American Journal of Clinical Nutrition*, 33 (1981): 914.

Bailey, B., and E. Collinson. "Dietary Sources of Fiber." *Journal of Human Nutrition*, 30 (1976): 303.

Balducci, L., C. Wallace, R. Khansur, R. B. Vance, Thigben, and C. Hardy. "Nutrition, Cancer, and Aging: An Annotated Review on Diet, Carcinogenesis, and Aging." *Journal of the American Geriatric Society*, 34, No. 2 (1986): 127–136.

Baron, J. A., et al. "A Randomized Controlled Trial of Low Carbohydrate, and Low Fat/High Fiber Diets for Weight Loss." *American Journal of Public Health*, 76, No. 11 (1986): 1293–1296.

Bijlani, R. L. "Dietary Fibre: Consensus and Controversy." *Progress in Food Nutritional Science*, 9, No. 3–4 (1985): 343–393.

Bistrian, B. R. "The Medical Treatment of Obesity." *Archives of Internal Medicine*, 141 (1981): 429–430.

Brender, J., et al. "Fiber Intake and Childhood Appendicitis." *American Journal of Public Health*, 75, No. 4 (April 1985): 399–400.

Brodribb, A. J. M., and C. Groves. "Effect of Bran Particle Size on Stool Weight." *Gut,* 19 (1978): 601.

Burkitt, D. P. "Effect of Dietary Fibre on Stools and Transit Time and Its Role in the Causation of Disease." *Lancet,* 2 (1972): 1408–1412.

Burkitt, D. P. "Varicose Veins, Deep Vein Thrombosis, and Haemorrhoids: Epidemiology and Suggested Aetiology." *British Medical Journal,* 2 (1972): 556–561.

Burkitt, D. P. "Hiatus Hernia: Is It Preventable?" *The American Journal of Clinical Nutrition,* 34 (March 1981): 428–431.

Burkitt, D. P. "Dietary Fiber: Is It Really Helpful?" *Geriatrics,* 37 (1982): 1119–1126.

Burkitt, D. P. "Fiber as Protective Against Gastrointestinal Diseases." *The American Journal of Gastroenterology,* 79, No. 4 (1984): 249–252.

Cohen, Z. "Alternatives to Surgical Hemorrhoidectomy." *Canadian Journal of Surgery,* 28 (May 1985): 230–231.

Committee on Nutrition in Medical Education. *Nutrition Education in the United States Medical Schools,* National Academy Press, 2101 Constitution Avenue N.W., Washington, D.C. (1985).

Crane, J. M., Amoury, R. and S. Hellerstein. "Hereditary Pancreatitis: Report of a Kindred." *Journal of Pediatric Surgery,* 8, No. 6 (December 1973): 893–900.

Cummings, J. H. "Dietary Fibre." *British Medical Bulletin,* 37, No. 1 (1981): 65–70.

Cummings, J. H., M. J. Hill, and D. J. Jenkins. "Changes in Fecal Composition and Colonic Function Due to Cereal Fiber." *American Journal of Clinical Nutrition,* 29 (1976): 1468.

Cummings, J. H., and A. M. Stephan. "The Role of Dietary Fibre in the Human Colon." *Canadian Medical Association Journal,* 123 (December 6, 1980): 1109–1114.

Davies, L. "Healthy Retirement." *Nursing Mirror,* 158, No. 5 (February 4, 1984): 22–24.

DiSogra, L. *Nutrition and Cancer Prevention: A Guide to Food Choices,* adapted by the National Cancer Institute (1985).

Drasar, B. S., and D. Irving. "Environmental Factors and

Cancer of the Colon and the Breast." *British Journal of Cancer*, 27 (1973): 167.

Edwards, C. H., et al. "Utilization of Wheat by Adult Man: Nitrogen Metabolism, Plasma Amino Acids and Lipids." *American Journal of Clinical Nutrition* (1971): 181–193.

Farris, R. P., et al. "Dietary Studies of Children from a Biracial Population: Intake of Carbohydrate and Fiber in Ten- and Thirteen-Year-Olds." *Journal of American College of Nutrition*, 4, No. 4 (1985): 421–435.

Fisher, N., et al. "Cereal Dietary Fiber Consumption and Diverticular Disease: A Lifespan Study in Rats." *American Journal of Clinical Nutrition*, 42, No. 5 (November 1985): 788–804.

Goodwin, P. "Cyclical Mastopathy, A Critical Review of Therapy." *British Journal of Surgery*, (September 1988) No. 75: 837.

Greenwald, P., E. Lanza, and G. A. Eddy. "Dietary Fiber in the Reduction of Colon Cancer Risk." *Journal of the American Diet Association*, 9 (September 1987): 117–188.

Hautvast, J. G. et al. "Nutrition and HDL in Children and Young Adults." *Preventive Medicine*, 12, No. 1 (January 1983): 44–46.

Heaton, K. W. "Are Gallstones Preventable?" *World Medicine*, 14 (1978): 21–23.

Heaton, K. W. "Western Diseases, Their Emergence and Prevention." *British Medical Journal*, 2 (1981): 47–59.

Heller, S. N., and L. R. Hackler. "Changes in the Crude Fiber Content of the American Diet." *American Journal of Clinical Nutrition*, 31 (1978): 1510–1513.

Hendren, W. H., J. M. Greep, and A. S. Patton. "Pancreatitis in Childhood: Experience with 15 Cases." *Archives of Internal Medicine*, 40 (1965): 132–145.

Hill, M. J. "Dietary Fat and Human Cancer." *Proceedings of the Nutrition Society*, 40 (1981): 15–19.

Hill, M. J., B. S. Drasar, and R. E. William. "The Relationship of Dietary Fiber to Colon Cancer." *Lancet*, 1 (1975): 533–535.

Hodges, R. E., and T. Rebello. "Dietary Changes and Their Possible Effect on Blood Pressure." *American Journal of*

Clinical Nutrition, 41, No. 5, (May 1985): 155–1162.

Jacobs, L. R. "Effect of Dietary Fiber on Colonic Cell Proliferation and Its Relationship to Colon Carcinogenesis." *Preventive Medicine,* 4 (July 1987): 566–571.

Jenkins, D. J. "Starchy Foods, Type of Fiber, and Cancer Risk." *Preventive Medicine,* 4 (July 1987): 545–553.

Kameda, H., et al. "Clinical and Nutritional Study on Gallstone Disease in Japan." *Japan Journal of Medicine,* 23 (May 1984): 109–113.

Kay, R. M. "Dietary Fiber." *Journal of Lipid Research,* 23 (1982): 221–241.

Kay, R. M., and A. S. Truswell. "Effect of Wheat Fiber on Plasma Lipids and Fecal Steroid Excretion in Man." *British Journal of Nutrition,* 37 (1977): 227.

Keys, A. "Fiber and Pectin in the Diet and Serum Cholesterol Concentration in Man." *Proceedings of the Society for Experimental Biology and Medicine,* 106 (1961): 555–558.

Manning, A. P. et al. "Wheat Fiber and the Irritable-Bowel Syndrome." *Lancet,* 2 (1977): 417–418.

McIntosh, E. "Nutrition Education in the Workplace." *Occupational Health Nursing,* 2 (December 1984): 646–648.

McPherson, Kay. "Fiber, Stool Bulk, and Bile Acid Output: Implications for Colon Cancer Risk." *Preventive Medicine,* 4 (July 1987): 540–544.

Miranda, P. and D. Horowitz. "High Fiber Diets in the Treatment of Diabetes Mellitus." *Annals of Internal Medicine,* 88 (1978): 482–486.

Modan, B., et al. "Low Fiber Intake as an Etiologic Factor in Cancer of the Colon." *Journal of the National Cancer Institute,* 55 (1976): 15–20.

Murphy, C. "Nutrition Education at the Worksite." *Nutrition News,* 45, (December 1983): 13–16.

National Center of Health Statistics. "Preliminary Findings of the First Health and Nutrition Examination Survey, 1971–1972, Anthropometric and Clinical Findings." Government Printing Office, Washington, D.C., Pub. No. 175-1229 (1975).

Pacy, P. J., et al. "High Fiber, Low Sodium and Low Fat Diet in White and Black Type 2 Diabetics with Mild

Hypertension." *Diabetes Resident*, 3, No. 6 (July 1986): 287–292.

Painter, N. S., A. Z. Almeida, and K. W. Colebourne. "Unprocessed Bran in Treatment of Diverticular Disease of the Colon." *British Medical Journal*, 2 (1972): 137–140.

Painter, N. S., and D. P. Burkitt. "Diverticular Disease of the Colon, a 20th-Century Problem." *Clinical Gastroenterology*, 4 (1975): 3–21.

Philipson, H. "Dietary Fiber in the Diabetic Diet." *Acta-Medica-Scandanavia* (Suppl). 671 (1983): 91–93.

Prynne, C. J., and D. A. T. Southgate. "Effects of a Supplement of Dietary Fiber on Feacal Excretion by Human Subjects." *British Journal of Nutrition* 41 (1979): 495.

Reddy, B. S. "Dietary Fiber and Colon Cancer: Epidemiologic and Experimental Evidence." *Canadian Medical Association Journal*, 123 (November 1980): 850–856.

Reddy, B. S. "Dietary Fiber and Colon Cancer: Animal Model Studies." *Preventive Medicine*, 4 (July 1987): 559–565.

Reuben, D., and B. Reuben. "*The Save Your Life Diet*." New York: Ballantine Books, 1976.

Rheinhold, J. G., et al. "Decreased Absorption of Calcium, Magnesium, Zinc, and Phosphorus by Humans Due to Increased Fiber and Phosphorus Consumption as Wheat Bread." *Journal of Nutrition*, 106 (1976): 495.

Ritchie, J. A., S. C. Truelove, and G. M. Ardran. "Propulsion and Retropulsion in the Human Colon Demonstrated by Time-Lapse Cinefluorography." *Gut*, 9 (1968): 735–736.

Rozovski, S. "Nutrition for Older Americans." *Aging*, Washington, D.C., U.S. Department of Health and Human Services, Administration of Aging. (April–May 1984): 499–563.

Salerno, M. "Nutrition for the Older Adult: Diet Needn't Be Hazardous to Health." *Occupational Health Nursing*, 33 (March 1985): 134–152.

Schire, V. "Heart Disease in Southern Africa with Special Reference to Ischaemic Heart Disease." *South African Medical Journal*, 45 (1971): 634–644.

Segal, I., A. Paterson, and A. R. Walker. "Characteristics and Occurrence of Appendicitis in the Black Population." *Journal of Clinical Gastroenterology*, 8 (October 1986): 530–533.

Segal, I., A. Solomon, and J. A. Hunt. "Emergence of Diverticular Disease in the Urban South African Black." *Gastroenterology*, 72 (1977): 215–219.

Shipman, R. T. "The Use of Dietary Fiber in the Management of Simple Childhood Idiopathic, Recurrent Abdominal Pain. Results of a Prospective Double Blind, Randomized, Controlled Trial." *American Journal of Diseases of Children*, 139, No. 12 (December 1985): 1216–1218.

Spiller, G., and H. Freeman. "Recent Advances in Dietary Fiber and Colorectal Diseases." *The American Journal of Clinical Nutrition*, 34 (June 1981): 1145–1152.

Stephan, A. M. "Should We Eat More Fiber?" *Journal of Human Nutrition*, 35 (1981): 403–414.

Story, J. A. "The Role of Dietary Fiber in Lipid Metabolism." *Advances in Lipid Research*, 18 (1981): 229–246.

Trowell, H., and D. P. Burkitt. "The Physiological Role of Dietary Fiber: A Ten-Year Review." *ASDC-Journal-Dent-Child*, 53, No. 6 (November–December 1986): 444–447.

Walker, A. R. "Diet and Bowel Diseases—Past History and Future Prospects." *South African Medical Journal*, 68 (August 1985): 148–152.

Walker, A. R., et al. "Appendicitis, Fibre Intake and Bowel Behaviour in Ethnic Groups in South Africa." *Postgraduate Medical Journal*, 49 (April 1973): 243–249.

Weinreich, J. "Dietary Fiber: Current Developments of Importance to Health." Discussion in *Heaton, K. W., ed.* London: John Libbey, 1978.

Appendix I

FOODS RICH IN DIETARY FIBER

FOOD SOURCE	Total dietary fiber (g/100 g)
Flours (wheat)	
Bran	44.0
Brown	7.87
Whole wheat	9.51
White, breadmaking	3.15
Breads	
Whole wheat	8.50
Brown	5.11
White	2.72
Breakfast cereals	
All-Bran	26.7
Puffed Wheat	15.41
Shredded Wheat	12.26
Cornflakes	11.0
Granola (mixed brands)	7.41
Grape Nuts	7.00
Sugar Puffs	6.08
Special K	5.45
Rice Krispies	4.47

FOOD SOURCE	Total dietary fiber (g/100 g)
Cookies and Crackers	
Crispbread, rye	11.73
Crispbread, wheat	4.83
Oat cakes	4.00
Matzo	3.85
Chocolate (½ coated)	3.50
Chocolate (fully coated)	3.09
Semisweet	2.31
Ginger	1.99
Shortbread	1.66
Wafers (filled)	1.62
Leafy vegetables	
Broccoli tops (boiled)	4.10
Brussels sprouts (boiled)	2.86
Cabbage (boiled)	2.83
Onions (raw)	2.10
Cauliflower (boiled)	1.80
Lettuce (raw)	1.53
Legumes	
Peas, frozen (raw)	7.75
Peas, processed (canned, drained)	7.85
Peas, garden (canned, drained)	6.28
Beans, baked (canned)	7.27
Beans, string (boiled)	3.35
Root vegetables	
Parsnips (raw)	4.90
Carrots, young (boiled)	3.70
Rutabagas (raw)	2.40
Turnips (raw)	2.20
Potato	
Chips	11.9
Raw	3.51
Canned (drained)	2.51
French fried	3.20

FOOD SOURCE	Total dietary fiber (g/100 g)
Fruits	
Pears (peel only)	8.59
Pears (flesh only)	2.44
Grapes	4.40
Apples (peel only)	3.71
Apple (flesh only)	1.42
Guavas (canned, fruit and syrup)	3.64
Peaches (flesh and skin)	2.28
Strawberries (raw)	2.12
Strawberries (canned, fruit and syrup)	1.00
Rhubarb (raw)	1.78
Bananas	1.75
Plums (flesh and skin)	1.52
Cherries (flesh and skin)	1.24
Mangoes (canned, fruit and syrup)	1.00
Grapefruit (canned, fruit and syrup)	0.44
Mandarin oranges (canned, fruit and syrup)	0.29
Nuts	
Peanuts	9.30
Brazils	7.73
Preserves	
Peanut butter	7.55
Mincemeat	3.19
Pickle	1.53
Strawberry jam	1.12
Plum jam	0.96
Marmalade	0.71
Beverages (concentrated)	
Cocoa	43.27
Instant coffee	16.41
Hot chocolate	8.20
Coffee and chicory essence	0.79

Adapted from D.A.T. Southgate, B. Bailey, E. Collinson et al. *Journal of Human Nutrition* 30 *(1976):* 303.

Appendix II

Diet Information and Suggestions for a High-Fiber Diet

By increasing the fiber of your diet, stool size will be increased and the time food waste remains in your colon will be shortened. A *possible* adverse effect of this diet may be increased gas. This is sometimes accompanied by bloating, abdominal pain, and diarrhea. To minimize this side effect, gradually increase the fiber in your diet and drink five to eight cups of fluid per day. Include exercise in your daily schedule to help increase bowel tone, such as a brisk walk for one-half hour or more.

Major Sources of Fiber in the Diet:
Fruits and vegetables with edible skins and seeds are highest in fiber. Other than this difference, fresh, cooked, frozen, and canned all have virtually the same amount.

Bread, cereal, whole-grain breads and crackers, breakfast cereals with "bran" in the name, or which include whole-grain flour in ingredients list are highest.

FOOD GROUP	FOODS	AMOUNT	CRUDE FIBER CONTENT
MILK		Minimum 2 cups/day	0
VEGETABLE		Minimum 3 serv/day	
	Artichoke	100 gm.	2.4
	Beans, dry, cooked	½ cup	4.2
	Beans, lima	½ cup	1.8
	Beans, snap or wax	½ cup	1.0
	Beets, cooked	½ cup, diced	0.7
	Broccoli	⅔ cup	1.5
	Brussels sprouts	⅔ cup	1.6
	Cabbage, raw	1 cup	1.0
	Carrots, raw	1 large or 2 small	1.0
	Cauliflower	⅞ cup	1.0
	Celery	2 large stalks	0.6
	Collards	½ cup	0.8
	Corn, whole, canned	½ cup	0.7
	Cucumber, raw	½ medium	0.3
	Eggplant	½ cup	0.9
	Green beans	½ cup	0.6
	Kale	¾ cup	1.1
	Lentils	⅔ cup	1.2
	Lettuce, iceberg	3½ oz.	0.5
	Mushrooms, canned	½ cup	0.6

Okra	8-9 pods	1.0
Onions, raw	1, 2½" diameter	0.6
Parsnips	½ cup	2.0
Peas, green	⅔ cup	2.0
Radishes, red, raw	10 small	0.7
Rutabaga	½ cup	1.1
Soybeans, mature, cooked	½ cup	1.6

FRUIT

Encourage dried fruits such as raisins, apricots, peaches, pineapple, prunes, dates, figs, fig cookies, coconut, fruit jams made from berries, marmalade.

	3 or more serv/day	
Apple, raw, whole	1 medium	1.5
Apple, dried	⅛ cup	0.8
Applesauce	⅓ cup	0.5
Apricots, dried	4 halves	0.9
Avocado	½	1.6
Banana	1 small	0.5
Banana, dehydrated powder	3½ oz.	2.0
Berries	½ cup	1.3 or 2.6
Cantaloupe	¼ of 5" diameter	0.3
Currants	¾ cup	3.4
Dates, dried	½ cup	2.1
Figs	3 small	1.2
Figs, dried	2 small	1.6
Fruit cocktail, canned	½ cup	0.4
Grapefruit	½ of 4" diameter	0.2

FOOD GROUP	FOODS	AMOUNT	CRUDE FIBER CONTENT
FRUIT			
	Grapes, Thompson, seedless	½ cup	0.2
	Orange, raw	2½" diameter	0.5
	Peach	1 medium	0.6
	Peaches, canned	2 medium halves	0.4
	Peaches, dried	⅓ cup	0.9
	Pear	½ medium	1.4
	Pears, canned	2 small halves	0.6
	Pears, dried, cooked	3½ oz.	2.9
	Pineapple	1 slice	0.4
	Pineapple, canned	1 slice	0.3
	Prunes, dried	5 medium	0.8
MEAT		6 oz. a day	0
FAT		Moderation	0
OTHER CATEGORIES			
Desserts			
	Blackberry pie	⅙ of 9" pie	3.0
	Apple pie	⅙ of 9" pie	0.6
	Chocolate meringue pie	⅙ of 9" pie	0.3
	Cherry pie	⅙ of 9" pie	0.2
	Cake (no icing)	1 piece	0.1

Nuts and Seeds

Cashews, roasted	30 to 40 nuts	0.1
Chestnuts, dried	100 grams	2.5
Coconut	100 grams	3.9
Macadamia nuts	100 grams	2.5
Peanuts with skin	100 grams	
	(approx. 5 tbsp.)	2.4
Pecans	100 grams (3½ oz.)	2.3
Sunflower seed kernels	100 grams (3½ oz.)	3.8
Walnuts	100 grams	1.7

St. Luke's Regional Medical Center, Nursing Division, Boise, Idaho

Index